FALLING AWAY

ALSO BY DAVID BANNING

NON-FICTION:
An A-Z of Cumbria and the Lake District on Film
Boundary Songs: Notes from the Edge of the Lake District National Park

EDITOR/CONTRIBUTOR:
From Tarmac to Towpath: Excursions into Lockdown

DOCUMENTARY:
Song of the Road
Becoming the Path Itself (The Dreams of Exiled Souls)
West Cumbria Mining: The Silence between Shadows

FALLING AWAY

David Banning

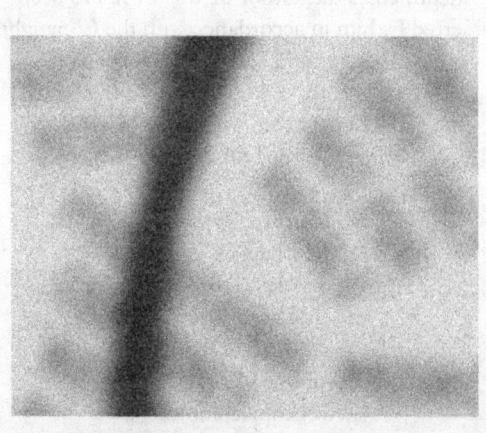

Chroma Editions

A Chroma Editions Book

First published 2023

Copyright © 2023 David Banning

The right of David Banning to be
identified as the author of this work has been
asserted by him in accordance with the Copyright,
Designs and Patents Act, 1988.

Cover image *Atelier I* by Iain Sharpe
(Pen & Pencil on Paper, 2022)

Chroma Editions
2 Chapel Close
Hest Bank
Lancashire
LA2 6DR
Telephone 07929 930001
www.chromaeditions.com
@ChromaEditions

ISBN: 978-1-8380915-5-2

A CIP catalogue record for this book is available
from the British Library

CONTENTS

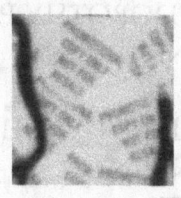

BATDANCE	13
DINO FACTS	14
TURMOIL	16
SICK OBSESSION	17
THE CHICKEN LADY	18
LAZARUS, THE PRINCE OF DARKNESS	21
A TACTICAL SURRENDER	25
THE BAREST OF NICKS	28
A TAHITIAN MASTERPIECE	29
THE CROW'S NEST	30
A MYSTERIOUS INTERCOURSE	34
MIMICKING CONCEPTUAL ART	36
WHO'S THIS THEN?	37
A SICKLY ATMOSPHERE	39
I DON'T WANNA GO DOWN TO THE BASEMENT	40
FATHER DIAMOND	42
THE ROUNDABOUT	44
FUCK POLITICS	45
SEXUAL POETICS	47
TAPIOCA DE WANKEUR	48
GENERATION X	52

THE WORLD AT WAR	55
SPACE DEMENTIA	57
WI-FI EVANGELISM	64
SINNER	65
RHYTHMIC GRACE	67
THE BALLAD OF DOROTHY PARKER	68
I'M DOING JASON!	77
A LAST BEAUTY	80
CHAINED TO THE POT WASH	82
MASKED DISCONTENT	85
BREAKING POINT	86
THERE ARE ONLY ARTISTS	88
BACK INTO THE PIT	90
SEALED WITH A KISS	91
DANGER ZONE	93
ZERO HOURS	101
WATFORD GAP	103
HOT OR COLD WITH THAT?	104
THE MUD-CHOKED WASTELAND	105
SIMPLY BOTIFUL	107
OL' BLUE EYES	110
JUICY COUTURE	113
SLEEPING ELEPHANTS	118
LA SCHIAVONA	121
THE INFINITE HAZE	126
LEAVE, HUH?	129

"I broke out into a sweat and the worlds of Rilke, the poet, entered my brain -- his notion that we are all of us born with a letter inside us, and that only if we are true to ourselves, may we be allowed to read it before we die."

Douglas Coupland, *Generation X: Tales for an Accelerated Culture*

when I left you at the Coronet this morning
you said that your happiness was gone
but the hum of voices somehow brings me back here
though there's no happiness and there's no love...

The Clientele, *Emptily Through Holloway*

We lingered beside the bed, alone in some form of windy cave, averting eyes, trying to compose ourselves. In the end I couldn't think of anything to say, so I skipped the queue for final goodbyes. With the curtains drawn, the ward clerk came and led us into a white-washed room opposite his desk. Facing each other in a semi-circle, nobody said a word.

Consumed by a dismal tune filtering among the graves, the sound of fading music filled the space like an unnamed sorrow. I kept mulling it over, trying to process the last few hours. On the drive down I thought I'd be able to take it all in my stride. But the truth is, a great silence had frozen the world in a huge sky, the size of our very souls.

PART ONE

| London / Brighton 2001 - 2003 |

The Disintegration Loops

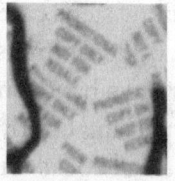

BATDANCE

Back in the late 80s, when I was growing up, I often used to experience a phenomenon known as 'sleep falling.' On several occasions I awoke abruptly from the depths just as the silent shadows were unfolding their wings. Usually triggered by an involuntary muscle movement called a hypnic jerk, the sensation occurred when my body was in a state of deep relaxation in preparation for sleep (known as the hypnagogic state). It turned out to be nothing new or weird even, plenty of others regularly experienced the sense of falling in their sleep too. There were various scientific explanations, but I always preferred the story from Greek mythology about the Oneiroi dream demons. It was thought the dark-winged spirits (*daimones*) resided on the coasts of the western seas. From their cavernous home in Erebus, the land of eternal darkness, they emerged each night like a colony of Chiroptera. Responsible for providing both visions and nightmares, the Oneiroi sought to play tricks on mortals by making them believe they were falling in dreams.

Nearly two decades later, another collection of bats took flight again. They appeared on a warm summer evening at the top of Wansfell. I had the summit crags to myself for once. There with eyes fixed on the sudden grace floating off over Windermere and beyond to the inter-tidal mudflats of Morecambe Bay. On the way over the beck, I had picked my steps carefully on the sharp descent to a small stone bridge immersed in trees, briars and bushes. Here I observed a handsome dipper stalking the riverbed, sometimes pausing briefly to bob up and down on an outjutting of small rocks with that familiar habit of theirs. Up towards the entrance to Townfoot Byre, tucked away under the shelter of a fine-looking red acer and mature golden beech hedging. Eventually, I made my way along Holbeck Lane past Townend and the Old Post Office before accessing the open fell through a wooden gate off Nanny Lane. As the sky turned scarlet and drew close, I shut my eyes and began the tumble toward the outline of fells stretching from Helvellyn along Fairfield to Rydal and Red Screes with the distinctive white-washed Kirkstone Pass Inn slightly behind on my right hand side. I woke sharply bathed in a soft blue light with the sound of a distorted string bend and piano key on a loop.

DINO FACTS

The first time I Googled it there was lots of God crap, the number for a help line and an article from a 1912 Journal of the American Medical Association about several cases of fatal salt poisoning in China. What I'd really wanted to find wasn't there. So I tried rephrasing it. But it didn't seem to matter whatever I put. I guess nobody really knows what will happen after the rhythm deadens and everything stops. I always had a talent for keeping secrets though. I mean the biggest one I kept from practically everyone. The problem was afterwards I couldn't handle any loud noises, smiles, tantrums and coochy fucking coo nonsense. Increasingly, all I had to offer in return was either a blank pitiless face or a pathetic scratch of the head.

Daydreams came thick and fast and could not be more contradictory. Most of them featured transparent blue skies and the Undercliff. In one of them, it was high tide with the horizon flooded in a warm, velvety coloured light as torches of spray kicked up against the battlements. I stood on the deck of the thick parapet transfixed by its beauty. Memories flowing like the cars on the coastal road high above. As I walked toward the sea wall, I watched a line of them drop anchor off the shore. On board, drums played an incessant rhythm, beating out four beats to the bar with an accent on the first beat. The sound of the waves and the drums solidified into celestial twins. Then, from the middle of the boat a solitary figure crept in silence dragging a flimsy piece of rope. With every heartbeat the drums got louder until a glowing moon red-hot through and through froze the dirty pretty things on the blackened shores of death.

Other reveries brought peculiar combinations. Like a golden god with a thick mane of hair, sparkling blue eyes, slim physique and a bluesy yelp riding a Smilodon. An extinct sabre-toothed cat belonging to the Pliocene period that once ranged over the entire American continent. A couple of trapped dinosaurs, the pair had been incarcerated in a long white hospital corridor. Just like the ones that are steeped in cocktails of blood, alcohol, urine, faeces and disinfectant. At first, I had no idea why the dynamic duo should be infiltrating my subconscious. But then I thought about it for a moment and remembered buying a packet of cereal with some free 3D 'Dino Fact Cards' inside.

That still didn't explain where the rock icon had sprung from...

TURMOIL

Hearing and seeing things, sometimes I couldn't open doors or sleep. With hints of Sinclair's 'ghost imagery without a border' a presence of developing fluid started to leave my bed every day, clinging on to the bedframe to hoist itself up. I used to watch the thing hopping from one foot to the other trying to get a leg into my jeans. Nervously, trialling a few steps, probing the floor with spindly toes outstretched. Disaster almost struck straight away, but it just about managed to swerve the Tascam 4-track at the last moment, before crunching into a pile of CD cases instead. Little shards of plastic almost punctured bare feet, but of course it couldn't feel a thing. Dark clouds of turmoil swooped down and gathered as the ghost shut its eyes, embracing the gloom for a brief moment. With hands crossed over, the thing lowered its head slowly onto them until they were only supported by a scrawny pair of knees.

After a while the ghostly visitation faded and I began to exist again. I knew this because I had become transfixed by the spaced out teeth on a wide-tooth comb, like a silent fiction on the bedroom carpet. Staring in mute composure, I bent down and scooped it off the floor. But the sudden movement only caused my vision to blur before the comb fell into obscurity again.

SICK OBSESSION

Home was a rented two-bed council flat in South East London. I shared it with an occasional flatmate who spent most of his time away seeing the rest of the world. He'd secured a cushy number at one of the big swanky museums and always seemed to have loads of flexi and time off. I'm not sure how, but he got the place through a special hush-hush deal with a friend of his. Seeing as the record company paid such paltry wages, I couldn't afford to turn down the offer of dirt cheap rent (about £160 a month). The flat was in one of those concrete monstrosities put up on the cheap in the early post-war building bonanza. We knew it wouldn't be long before the bulldozers moved in. There were rumours in the 70's that members of Squeeze and Dire Straits had been brothers in arms on the five-storey block. I'd gone there just as the clicks started to render the outer world dim and dead. With the noise of Old Bone's shutter falling, the music stopped when time became bleached into the brick walls holding us all inside the estate.

Visitors were rare even before I began slipping in and out of the 'dead moods.' Sometimes a few colleagues came round to reminisce and medicine anyone brave enough with massive blocks of resin or bags of sweet-smelling numbness. Somehow the sparkles of old times dissipated with the black smoke threatening to darken all of our lives. Afterwards, there were usually a few unexpected left-overs. Once, I found a bottle of my flatmate's CK One floating in a pool of brown vomit in the bathroom sink. Holding my breath, I just ran the tap and waved goodbye to the scent of a generation. Positioning a cold flannel over my face, I swirled round a few cups of mouthwash and tried expunging the night's excess. I had no idea what had actually happened creeping nervously toward the kitchen, mind and body temporarily revived. Pulling down on the door handle, I held my breath again, before entering a wasteland colder than moonlight. Gazing at the ragtime army of bottles and cans, a frightful banquet had fouled the night. This new Chamber of Horrors looked so real I wanted to throw up myself. Fragments of broken glass, smashed plates, corks and bottle tops created a colourful mosaic as if the madness had erupted and poured across the room. Ashtrays overflowed with the residue of sombre flames. Making an enemy of the future, I had entered Withnail's slow drift 'into the arena of the unwell.' With the back of my right hand I swept aside a stack of polystyrene takeaway boxes only to discover a glinting Medusa-like raft set adrift in the sink. Barely seaworthy riding the waves, a large pizza box clothed in several slices of doner meat was about to capsize. Shaking and about to be sick, I had a sudden urge to consult with Google again.

THE CHICKEN LADY

Forays downstairs or outside grew increasingly rare in the daytime. I felt much safer going out under the cover of night. Mainly to try and avoid a group of about six or seven that regularly hung out by the door entry system. Sullen and mean, they loitered near the bottom of the stairs demanding cigarettes, spare change or simply trying to barge their way in. One of them I nicknamed, The Chicken Lady. She had a large, pale round face with cold fish eyes and pockmarked skin. She bore an uncanny resemblance to Tin Tin or Jimmy Somerville, small and bony with legs shaped like Twiglets and straw coloured hair tied back in a thin wiry strip. Her shrill, nasal voice penetrated all the way through. She was a skilful operator, packed full of small town charm. Anyone would do a doubletake at the sight of her stomping up and down the pavement with an abnormally wide and heavy stride. Head bobbing up and down spasmodically like a dipper's dark body plumage in pursuit of any passers-by. Sometimes, I watched folk go to extraordinary lengths just to avoid her, either scampering round the other side of the roundabout or stepping out onto the road causing drivers to slam on the brakes. Always in close attendance, a tall, slim guy held a mobile tight against his ear and kept an eye out. I imagine he would rather have been carrying the crusade somewhere in the Blue Mountains, seeking out beats infused with the poetry of disappointment. Occasionally, the Chicken Lady dropped something into one of his coat pockets. After a month or two, her belly started to bulge outwards.

The others looked a bit younger than them, I'd guess around twenty or thirty at a push. They formed part of a mostly male collective who spent their time like ghosts in the daylight, drifting up and down the estate pathways until late afternoon. Usually, a small hard core with the odd new arrival returned later on. Clutching several cans of Red Stripe, which on the odd occasion might inspire an impromptu group sing-along. During these moments I used to envy their camaraderie and apparent dedication to one another. Spending many a bored evening watching them all sat on the playground benches from the relative safety of the balcony. No doubt their hearts were as black as the coats on their backs. But there was something almost divine about the way they huddled together as one. Laughing gregariously ripping open beer cans that foamed up all over each other, they seemed blissfully unaware of any real sense of time or spatial relations.

On the night I moved in, my first encounter had been with a little old lady. She was clothed in a long and threadbare overcoat with a large, but faded lime green headscarf wrapped tight. She called me a racist after an incident in the doorway. It happened during several attempts to drag a few heavy boxes of books from the hire van towards the entrance. Pausing briefly to set down one of the larger ones, I searched my pockets for the entry fob to swipe in. Unfamiliar with the ruthless speed of the mechanism, I didn't anticipate it swinging back quite so sharply. Striving to ghost-in behind me, a loud gasp punctured the air as the door almost knocked the old lady clean over. Catching a glimpse of a swaying arm in the murky hallway windows, I turned to offer assistance immediately. Pulling at the heavy door, I heard the tail end of her anguish. A disembodied mouth was still spewing out a volley of insults that seemed to hang there in the darkness, reminding me a little of Beckett's *Not I* - another 'organ of emission'. There I was, a white, postmodern mélange, ignored by history yet bound up with Stuart Hall's 'Euro-scepticism and Little Englander nationalism whose sugar flowed through English blood and rotted English teeth.'

Unerringly, as I tried to help the old lady shuffle inside, a trace of gilt from a lonesome front tooth started to wink at me under the glow from the bottom of the stairwell. Apart from the enormous headscarf, I noticed she had a pair of chapped lips that made her mouth look uncomfortable.

Her snappish tone increased, before I tried to calm proceedings with my hands, "OK, OK, please *stop*, look I'm really sorry for the door, I'm new here and didn't see you behind me…"

That seemed to quiet things briefly before she coughed from the bottom of her ribcage. An executioner's silence imbued the stairwell. Then, as if powered by a clockwork motor, she started cursing again; only this time it attracted a small pocket of the finger lickin' coterie, who hurried over towards us. They laughed and chased one another, throwing stones in puddles where the raindrops glittered. Eyes frozen in the timeless glow of the stairwell, I stood back, cleared my throat and made my excuses to the old lady who appeared to have entered a trance in the doorway. It was time to begin my escape. Embarrassed by the legacy of distilled Englishness, I bounded up the stairs vaulting discarded Rubicon cans and chicken bones submerged in a pool of piss.

LAZARUS, THE PRINCE OF DARKNESS

Not surprisingly, the neighbour I saw most was a skinny middle-aged guy who lived next door. He always looked completely knocked out of his mind on something or other especially when his head kept falling to one side. He had wayward eyes fixed with a sadness that ebbed and flowed like the deep. A washed-out complexion and twisted mouth, spoke of the hazards of addiction, while his hands would often swing out randomly from the elbow. Although he had a gentleness that marked him out as someone a bit different, someone who had lost whatever nerve they had in the first place. His gaze, cold and deep matched the random stories he tried to tell with a nasal whine that ended up in a sort of strangulated cough. I usually rounded off any of these outpourings with a bemused "Yeah" or "I know what you mean." His filthy jogging bottoms once black, now faded to a colour only a Landscape painter might recognise were covered in marks that radiated a subtle, but dangerous smell. In the silent shadows slumped over the balcony's edge, it was as if poisoned angels had been summoned to grapple with his beaten down soul. One of the only vague bits of sense I ever got out of him had something to do with the temperature of baking bread. I shrugged and turned my palms up, "Bread? Yeah, I know what you mean."

Comfortably numb like its owner, a small mongrel named Ralph usually remained by his side. Mostly white in colour except for a black patch covering his right eye and ear, the poor little mutt's sad puppy dog eyes and pointy-ears must have provided the only real companionship and warmth, especially during bitterly cold winter days and nights. Whenever my neighbour was awake long enough I noticed how he seemed to enjoy observing all the comings and goings near the roundabout below.

"Reckons he hears voices" he said on one occasion leaning over the balcony with his slippers almost off the floor. He was trying to get a glimpse of the guy everyone called Lazarus, the so-called prince from another planet. About 5ft tall with a heavy limp, Lazarus always wore a baggy, grey tracksuit with brown trainers replete with red and yellow laces. Meandering almost corpse-like around the estate, he ducked in and out of the foliage if ever anyone saw him. Beneath the reddish candles of night a strong, musky scent gave him away whenever plumes of smoke billowed out from the bushes. Like Dante, down among the damned, Lazarus lurked directly beneath our flat. Except his nocturnal episodes must have cast dark shadows over everyone. Initially, I had no idea where all the noise was coming from. Casting aspersions upstairs, until a note came through the door detailing the truth. It said to ask the council about our diurnal interloper. I think it was Tom Waits who once said 'there's always some Boo Radley type we're compelled to perceive through a keyhole.' And not long after the note, the secret history of our Prince of Darkness started to unravel. Almost every night Lazarus embarked on midnight wanderings, leaving his stereo up at full volume while the loud vibrations from his subwoofers crashed through our floorboards, forming a hypnotic spell often into the early hours. The opening notes of Handel's *Messiah* usually triggered proceedings off, but any oratorios were soon replaced with the harsh raspy buzz of AM radio.

He offered other gifts too. Namely, a huge collection of bric-a-brac pilfered during the same excursions. Sometimes, whenever he brought a fresh collection back I heard him pounding nails into hardwood accompanied by the operatic giggles of child-like laughter. Most of the left-overs were filthy and broken beyond repair though, rejected and left to rot by the bins or underneath the railway arches. Often, I wondered whether he might be attempting to build an island of whimsy whenever I passed the ever-expanding assemblage of bricks, pallets, bottles, wire mesh and corrugated iron piled high outside his front door. Maybe he would surprise everyone one day and reveal a unique sculptural form, similar to the giant, inverted ice cream cones in the centre of Watts. Some kind of symbol for the neglected and under-resourced mental health services, where junk can still cast a spell. Or perhaps he was constructing a new Mothership to replace the whole estate and transport any fellow believers and loose booty to Saturn or beyond.

I can't deny that the impact of Lazarus's psychotic behaviour became a constant strain on my nerves though, and soon enough I had to visit the Docs. They diagnosed acute insomnia and prescribed Temazepam, but not even the Jellies could block out a new hullabaloo from above.

The girl upstairs had obviously found a new partner, and they began cementing their blooming relationship long into the early hours - an exhausting schedule both for them and for me. To compound the overall sense of despair during the nightly 2-4am subwoofer-fests, a series of rampant high pitched shrieks easily cut through the din below, flooding into my consciousness...at first I thought it might be intruders, but when the groans became faster and yet more intense, I realised that nature was taking its course. Sometimes I thought they must be doing real harm to one another. Unfortunately an emergency cocktail of pills and ear plugs couldn't drown out the frantic moans or anaesthetise the tumultuous decibel level. When Ralph started to join-in, howling and wailing through the bedroom wall to my left, I could only seek salvation in Thomas Fuller's famous piece of folk wisdom. After a couple of months of being hemmed in on all sides, thankfully an eerie cease fire broke out. It happened after we finally managed to contact the council who got onto Lazarus's senior case worker. Stuck in the system, they must have given him more powerful medication and yet another final warning.

Despite the daytime void caused by severe insomnia, all the early morning antics became just another brick in the estates' deadening wall. Days, weeks and months passed without objects or interruption. I didn't care. My bootlaces were slowly winding around a broken mast. Any sudden knocks at the front door just meant that the weasels were closer. Comfort and silence rooted in the neon glow of a giant roadside clown, where the pink-and-gold porte-cochère is most exquisite. In this minimalist and noncomplex life, I fixed myself on the floor like an unclaimed autumn leaf. Wherever it had been before, everything seemed very different now. In only a short space of time, a change had come. With the same self-destructive and impulsive state as Coupland's 'Exercised Young Man,' I had quit my job and abandoned the big-brained netherworld of disinterested Trellick-chic. Now I had thrown a sledgehammer into the screen. Mainly to try and contain the ever-threatening teeming black scrawl.

A TACTICAL SURRENDER

I guess it all started with Beckham's penalty against Argentina on my last day. The time had come to quit the record company, Hunter S. Thompson's bastardised 'cruel and shallow money trench.' Not so independent after the corporate subsidies were allowed to bankroll the long plastic hallways. I'd already been daydreaming in the upstairs office for a good hour or two, so I decided to decamp somewhere else for a bit.

"Seeing as there's nothing more for me to do, I'll

grab an early lunch if that's ok?"

My boss picked up a silver zippo off her desk and started twizzling it round and round, before lighting up a Marlboro Light. Then she sat back in a swivelling chair with her legs crossed nodding without looking up.

"Thanks, I'll be in the Famous if anyone asks!" I didn't hang around in case she changed her mind.

I picked up a pack of cigs and skipped down the staircase poking my head over the mass of boxes hiding Tracey, the new Aussie on reception. Waving goodbye as she buzzed me out, I headed round the corner past Snappy Snaps to a small newsagent on the Fulham Road. Pausing on the pavement, I pulled up the sides of my t-shirt and scratched at the filth of the city. Held by mind-forged manacles I looked up at the slanting sun and thought of *Murphy's* opening line - 'The old forever new things in a slow fade to freedom.'

Strangely, the roads around the market stalls seemed deserted, as I made my way heading north towards the bland, almost blacked out frontage. Situated opposite a church, the pub had the visage of a strip joint. Inside, a number of large mirrors spray painted gold hung from baroque-themed wallpaper, spreading pomp and a castle-like ambience with symmetrical arrangements in black, silver and red. Soft light from light fittings with hanging droplets illuminated the bar and there was even a small garden behind a raised area where the interior stretched back.

A handful of withered adolescents who had arrived way too early occupied a set of dark mahogany stained chairs and tables. Breathing heavily, the rest of the clientele slumped around the bar on stools wearing red or white football shirts with mostly pale blue jeans.

They muttered to themselves and twirled coasters staring forlornly into pint glasses, as if the beer bubbles might provide answers to their afflictions. A couple of older looking ones drenched in their own cigarette smoke buried their heads intensely in the Racing Post. I stood near the till for a moment and studied the menu. It contained a regular selection of beers and wine, and even advertised a happy hour from 5-7pm featuring Cosmopolitans and Mojitos. Glancing at the food section, I noticed practically everything came with chips. Except the roasts of course, which boasted huge Yorkshires risen to heaven. I ordered a pint of 1664 and felt reasonably relaxed. This would definitely be home for the rest of the morning, perhaps the afternoon even. I didn't much care for the match; I just wanted to drink and chain-smoke my way to oblivion. Initially, I stayed on a stool by the bar. An attractive bar maid with a perfect counterfeit smile provided another good reason to stay there. She was tall and slim, brunette and foreign sounding. I couldn't make out where her accent came from. Not that it mattered anyway. Soon enough her colleagues cleared out all the furniture when the fans began filtering in like packs of rabid dogs, jostling one another around a selection of TV screens fixed on the walls in symmetrical patterns. Most were positioned high up into the corners of the raised section. The ones you had to assume giraffe-like status to crane your neck muscles just to catch fleeting glimpses of bootlaces. Suddenly someone from a crowd of suits announced their arrival with a raucous, "C'mon Ingerland!" that reverberated round the entire bar. As I strained to turn round they staggered into the back of my stool knocking the drink clean out of my hand. I swore under my breath just as a broad toothy grin on a pair of tubby red cheeks offered an apology. The group the guy was with lapped it all up, so I patted him on the shoulder and stood up straight, mouthing a "No worries mate" at the same time. With their annoying laughter still ringing in my ears, I decided a tactical retreat was in order. Thankfully, this unfortunate episode had also caught the attention of my favourite barmaid during her glass collecting duties. She sidled up straight away and offered a cloth while clearing the area to sweep up the broken glass. In honour of her diligence, I promptly approached the bar again ordering three more pints and a drink for her. The surrender of the stool had been inevitable. Moments later, I found solace in a tiny ledge abutting the raised section just big enough to fit all my drinks on.

'THE BAREST OF NICKS'

I clung onto the ledge for a while absorbing the slings and arrows, while a refrain from the jukebox, 'Deep ceded urban decay, Deep ceded urban decay' reverberated over everyone's heads. Filthy and futile, it seemed like a perfect embodiment for where I was headed. Even though I recoiled at the grating machismo, the anonymity amidst the chaos of the baying mob was exactly what I needed. I got into the drink and dug myself in, hammering away at the Nokia's buttons playing Space Impact, or typing out spurious texts of utter gibberish to myself, just to look like I had something 'going on.' Always in my most studious and monumental pose, particularly if any females just so happened to glance over. Any speculative dreams were soon dashed by a collective volley hurled at the screens above. Announcing the arrival of both teams onto the pitch, an exuberant five or six tradesman formed a dis-coloured blur of bibs and braces directly in front of my stronghold. Their clothes resembled rainbows dragged through the mud. With only moments to go before kick-off, no one could hear any sound. In unison, everyone vented their anger at Tweedle-dum and Tweedle-dee, a pair of rotund bar staff dressed black as a tar-barrel. Initially they searched extensively under the bar, before having to brave the tables and chairs of the jeering ensemble. Not that it made much difference when they eventually found the control, for scarcely anything could be heard above the pandemonium.

The match's crucial moment arrived just before half-time. Predictably, the game between two great old sporting foes proved to be a tense affair. It was being played under the lights at Japan's newly built Sapporo Dome stadium. With the time difference, it was a bit odd watching an evening kick off during our own lunchtime. 'The barest of nicks' is how one commentary described the trip on Michael Owen, the English centre forward who won the decisive spot-kick. It provided 'Golden Balls' (a nickname given to David Beckham by his wife, Posh Spice) with the chance for national redemption, after his petulant sending off against the same opposition in France four years earlier.

A TAHITIAN MASTERPIECE

After the match ended, the mob spilled out onto the Fulham Road. I decided to make my excuses at the same time, stumbling over a small green bottle edging out of the doorway onto the pavement. It rolled slowly towards the gutter like a worm devouring the dead. It came to rest beside a group of multi-coloured recycling bins across the road by the church. Perched on top, a solitary jackdaw eyed a crumpled bag of biscuits taunting him from the middle of the road. Under a flaming sun its head bobbed up and down until the traffic squashed the packet to a pulp. Not even a crumb of happiness was left. I crept away into the eye of a multitude rushing along to bright blue horizons.

I found a window seat at Nero's and texted my boss. I explained that I'd be back to clear out my desk and say goodbyes in around half an hour. A large Americano and a packet of cocoa wafers later, I started to feel a bit better. Ordering another coffee, I settled back and stared at the set of lights opposite. The reds, greens and ambers blended into one other, while an endless stream of cars, lorries and cyclists whirred past like waves on a beach. Everywhere I looked people ebbed and flowed in relentless rhythm. Ransacked by a sadness that closes over all of us like the terminal stages of some degenerative disease, Gauguin's huge 1897 Tahitian masterpiece sprung to mind. Supposedly a culmination of all his own thought, 'Seeing they see not, hearing they hear not.'

THE CROW'S NEST

I eventually made it back to the office around 4ish. Tracey laughed at my bungled attempts to mount the staircase while I pointed at her phone system lit up like a Christmas tree.

"What was the score drunkard?"

"I think it was 1-0 to Beckham" I offered in slight

return, a little out of breath.

Thankfully, Jenkins, the company's resident spiv and Head of Sales appeared at the top of the stairs. He promptly suggested a gab in the crow's nest. Jenkins always looked like someone who didn't quite know what they wanted but had gone through hell to get it. I followed him through the scent of spliff into the General Manager's office weaving past a sofa area surrounded by TVs and record decks. On the white walls a miscellany of framed platinum, gold and silver discs interlinked with magazine covers spoke of connections made and the fetishism of commodities.

"You're going to miss all this" he said with the same little smile he had used to introduce himself with on my first day. His slight frame ghosted off toward the far right-hand corner of the room where a couple of desks faced each other. Receiving nutrition from a platoon of overflowing ashtrays, a mixture of broad leaved and prickly plants gorged themselves on a rack above an oval shaped wooden coffee table. You couldn't miss the desk belonging to the Big Cheese; it was covered head-to-toe in post-it notes. It looked like some kind of sculptural diary or mini-graphic novel. Jenkins stood motionless next to a black bonded leather chair locked in an upright position. He reached above to pull open a trapdoor revealing a secret stairway to heaven. With Mahleresque larghetto, the spring loaded loft ladder unfolded in 3 sections. It had a wobbly mechanism that gave access to a triangular shaped area, enclosed on all sides by thick cardboard boxes, smothering any daylight trying to creep in through a bay window. Pushed tight against the walls, a couple of snug looking armchairs were dissected by a round filmy glass table overflowing with

CD's and vinyl. A red and white mini-fridge unceremoniously shoved-in beneath a stack of hi-fi separates added another layer to the built-in claustrophobia.

"Bit cramped in here I know, but still not a bad little bolt-hole!" said Jenkins, first up the steps. He was already pouring out a couple of healthy looking doubles by the time I dragged myself through the hatchway.

"Don't suppose you've ever seen the big man's army jeep have you?" he asked while at the same time using a crumpled post-it to wipe off a trail of dirt and mud from one of his desert boots.

"You should try a soft brush or an old toothbrush on that."

I leant forward in my chair, but something in the back of my head hurt as I leafed through a handful of 12" white labels left strewn across the carpet.

"It's one of those big American Second World War types; you know the open tops with massive wheels, high up off the floor. He had it sprayed in matt black!"

Sitting directly opposite, I noticed how his skinny frame twitched as he leant in closer and whispered through his yellow brown teeth…

"Mad bastard though…I braved going in it once with him, down to a studio on Ladbroke Grove. I'm not kidding, as he's driving he was laughing and trying to roll a joint at the same time! We were literally ALL OVER the place. Couldn't believe it, I just sat there with my eyes shut clinging on to the seat shitting myself!"

I straightened up, swung my legs round and tried to stretch out my feet, laughing and then coughing until my face must have turned a shade of purple.

A prism of colours broke through the cardboard and projected a Rothko onto the wall behind me. Jenkins wiped a corner of his mouth on the sleeve of a brand new navy Fred Perry polo shirt. Suddenly a mellow golden glow spread throughout the nest.

"Can't make it out later I'm afraid. Said I'd hook up with Les Hommes at the San Moritz Club. We're looking to put out a 7" or maybe an EP but we haven't decided just yet. Anyway, sorry about that…how about you - got anything lined up yet?" He asked.

"Hmm…"

"So that's a no then."

"Towards the end of Coupland's *Generation X* you'll find Linda's story, 'like a small yellow bird that can sing all songs.' Like her, I need to unlock the mechanisms - check it out sometime."

By 8pm I was locked in a cubicle of the gents with the ceiling of the Famous spinning like a set of dinner plates. After about twenty minutes slumped over the bowl, I finally broke out and just about managed to hold myself up at the sink. Taking fright at a face without lips in the mirror, I cupped both hands splashing cold water over and over until the day's pageant passed before my eyes. With each detail picked out in nightmarish charm, I returned to the table feeling much better and ready to begin again. More shots were clunked together as our tiny group laughed stupidly and dragged each other along, whilst some started to babble more and more gibberish after increasing their trips to the loos and back.

After that, I don't remember too much. All I know is that I woke up in unfamiliar surroundings next to Ali from Finance. I'd always liked her, but no matter how hard I tried to remember, I just couldn't recall anything about what had happened. She didn't give much away either on our slow walk to the station at Fortress Wapping. We said goodbye silent and a little gloomy at the bus stop. There didn't seem any point in exchanging numbers. I headed straight for the Golden Arches out of the Tube, making light work of a sausage and egg breakfast special. Around mid-day I ordered in a 13" Casa Pollo from Sorrento's with extra garlic bread, before rounding off the end of the beginning with a Chicken Dansak hand delivered from Boz Boz off the Broadway.

A MYSTERIOUS INTERCOURSE

As the dreaded Christmas period approached, I summoned up the courage to take a trip down to the folks place, hopeful that the roaring of the sea might provide brighter horizons. After taking an age to coax the car into life, I left at dusk on a drizzly Friday night with the light ebbing away just before it fell into interminable shade. On the outskirts of Brighton, I turned onto the A27, and skated through a couple of mini-roundabouts towards the undulating slopes near the university at Falmer. Rounding a tight right hand turn, the street lamps completely disappeared heading on to the South Downs. After a steady uphill section something glinted brightly in the headlights. Slowing to a crawl, whatever it was had sprawled and stretched itself out in the middle of the road. The dark, yet dreamlike vision unnerved me a little. The rising mist gathered from the middle of the fields and I could smell a bouquet of blood circling the car. Slowing to a halt, I switched off the engine somewhat hesitantly, before attempting to narrow my vision. Still I could not make out the mysterious shape in front. There it stood upright and unashamed, mystic eyes gleaming like the stars. Now they were fixed firmly onto the vehicle. Carefully, I pulled the hand break up with my left hand until it let out a gentle squeak. Glancing both ways without moving my head to make sure all the doors were locked. I moved my left hand forward in minute stages to turn the radio off; leaving the main beam locked on the road. I let out a deep breath that infused the interior before it struck the windscreen like a puff of smoke. I sat back with tightened shoulders and somewhere close by an owl hooted. Moments passed in the kind of creeping silence that returns forsaken souls to life. After picking at my nails under the steering wheel, I decided I had to do something. Suddenly the shadowy form advanced a few steps, before halting abruptly. Now it was within touching distance of the end of the bonnet. I sat motionless until a set of loud cries pierced a hole into the dark imaginings. Lit by a magnificent streak of moonlight the howls became louder and more magical. Even though my heart rushed for the abyss, I was completely enraptured by the mysterious intercourse playing out in front of me. The once gleaming eyes now resembled a deep and dark void spiralling into nothingness. Creeping closer, it brushed the bonnet grill, stretching its long neck towards the sky. Instinctively, I reached for the ignition key, but something prevented me turning the engine over. Instead, I reached across the passenger seat grasping for my phone. Making sure the light from the screen shone towards the floor mat after pressing the home button. I waited patiently for movement, before selecting the camera and positioning the phone at the top of the steering wheel. Seconds later, my mouth gaped after I snuck a peek at the screen. The image staring back didn't make any sense. Like the agony of a withered moon, white smoke whipped a haunted face that reflected onto the chalky cliffs rising above the ocean. Against the cold spring shadows of night, a ray of blue fell onto my lips. The same words repeated over and over, filling the road…

'The heat is closing in…'

MIMICKING CONCEPTUAL ART

Similar to Lazarus's psychotic wanderings back at home, night time was always the hardest whenever I stayed with the folks. I simply dreaded closing my eyes, for fear of what might happen. They lived in a small two bed bungalow, with the spare bedroom next to the bathroom. Unfortunately, this is where the nocturnal torture usually took place. According to mother, what began as just the odd incident every few weeks or so, had soon developed into a nightly pattern. And now, regular as clockwork, the shenanigans commenced with the sound of footsteps shuffling up and down the hallway around one in the morning. They got steadily louder until the bathroom doorknob screeched open. Then the cord for the light switch would be pulled up and down repeatedly while the door was half-open. It rarely closed properly during any of these carry-ons. Once woken, it was virtually impossible to drift off again. Earplugs were no use either. At least the ones I had were simply not up to the job, all I could do was bury my head further into the pillows.

One time, it must have been about half past four in the morning, the old man eventually fell asleep on the loo, pyjama bottoms soaked in urine with strands of toilet roll trailing along the walls spinning another tortuous web. The bathroom door had been revolving whimsically like a pair of rotating two-wings while the lights were going on and off every few seconds just like in the Turner Prize. The poor thing had no idea of the disruption he caused mimicking conceptual art. In the end, sleeping on the tiny sofa in the lounge proved to be the only method of combatting his increasingly hapless behaviour. Decamping there only exacerbated my lower back pain though, which dug in like a spade sinking into stone. Once impaired, sleep proved to be an exiled soul...

And then in a final coup de grace, he pulled the towel rail clean off the tiles with a cocaine crash so intense I contemplated picking it up and chucking it back at him. Instead, I leapt from the sofa and knocked a couple of times on the door, ironically closed for once.

"Dad, what's going on in there? You OK?"

I could barely recognise the sobs and bitter laughter coming from the other side.

WHO'S THIS THEN?

I looked up and baulked at an overcast sky. Staring out onto an endless waste of water, its vastness overwhelming, there was no way of telling where it ended and the horizon began. I remained motionless on the Undercliff for a little while longer, probably because there was no one else around. With the on-going night games, I enjoyed the freedom that a few stolen moments away from the folks brought. Often I would try to imagine what it would be like heading out into the void of the ocean, enchanted by the passing clouds, skipping like a stone at a fast disappearing England. Memories would speak like voices in the sigh of the waves, piling high above the chalky cliffs. Overhead, a soft and fuzzy sunset began to form, its orange hues sprawled across the sky with the blues cold and newly bright. Thoughts wandered back to the first time the old man failed to recognise me about a year or so earlier. Strangely, I didn't feel annoyed or even disappointed, just a resigned emptiness. Not that I'd ever been angry with him before, just a little weary whenever patience ran thin. I remembered watching him approach; wobbling along the pavement during his afternoon constitutional. Using a stick for balance, wrapped in an ill-fitting grey overcoat and chequered cap, treading the same stones, and the same piece of road like a weathered flag. I held the dog on a shorter lead, and approached slowly as he poked his stick at an empty cigarette packet tossed aside on the grass verge.

"Who's this then?" I said smiling at him. The dog's ears flattened and her bushy tail wagged like a propeller. He was breathing more heavily than usual and had stopped trying to move the bits of rubbish.

"Who's this then?" I tried again, letting the dog's lead unravel fully while my father audibly grimaced bending his right knee a little.

"You're lovely aren't you? My wife's got one just like you" he said, leaning in for a stroke. "And how old is this one?"

I coughed and tapped him gently on the arm.
"Dad, it's me…"

A SICKLY ATMOSPHERE

I always had a distant relationship with my father. He never really asked me what was going on. Come to think of it, we never really had the awkward sex chat; never really spoke about politics, music, art or life even. Sport was the only common ground between us, which we both hid behind during our moments together. And with time running out, neither of us would ever truly get to know who the other person really was. Suddenly I felt tired, rubbing my eyes whilst yawning widely to release a big breath into the world. Looking up, I watched a succession of clouds shift over, menacing like an apocalyptic nag. Turning round, I headed back towards the entrance of the pedestrian tunnel carved out underneath the White Cliff café. Drawing near to a trickle of steps I noticed two fresh bouquets. They were attached to a tall sign fixed into the pebbles on the beach. Curiously, they were hanging directly opposite the same bench where I'd sat alone for almost an hour the previous evening. A tiny refuge, after another fraught episode at the dinner table. Father had not been in his right mind and ended up having to change his trousers half way through. In need of some evening air, the pale glow of the moon had attracted me towards the shoreline. Once I scrambled down to the seawall battlement, the wind corrupt and masterful boomed around the spot where I huddled like a figure in a Munch drawing. In the sickly atmosphere, I watched a multitude of white horses crash-in against the sea wall, like an enemy striking with kidney-killing madness. My heart felt disturbed, as if something called from the middle of the ocean. A sadness rose with the waves, while a shimmering light parted a realm of mist and then rested, blown out in a final embrace. Upon returning to the folks' place, I caught the tail end of a local news report on the TV. It described how two young men had perished after being washed out to sea jumping from the Palace Pier. They were last seen clinging to each other in the ferocity of the waves. But a gale force nine dealt the pair a bitter fate.

I DON'T WANNA GO DOWN TO THE BASEMENT

On the drive back to London, I thought about my first so-called 'proper job' as a chip boy at Grant's Fish Bar on Upper High Street. I'd been doing various paper rounds throughout senior school, but turning sixteen brought the new prospect of earning more cash for records and beer. They were early evening shifts, between four thirty to around seven, three days a week. My workspace was hidden away down a rickety old wooden staircase directly beneath the fryer. In the basement mixing up the potatoes, I got paid to throw them into a giant cement mixer. The rumbler might have been big and cumbersome, but it had four good legs bolted to the floor. Made out of robust stainless steel and cast alloy it stood proudly next to the chipper, another hunk of steel, where my freshly rumbled spuds were poured into a large round container sitting on top of its main body. Perfectly shaped, the chips would then be tossed out of a guide chute on the side into a large plastic container, similar in looks to a laundry basket. They gave me a long white coat and a pair of wellies, mainly because the chips needed to be rinsed thoroughly after they had been cut.

Once washed through, I sent them upstairs in a squeaky lift that appeared to operate solely on its own terms. There were other pieces of equipment surrounding my workstation. These ranged from a group of chest freezers to a pair of tall ovens where whole chickens roasted on spits. The overpowering smell as they twizzled round used to make my stomach ache with desire. After sorting out the daily quota of spuds, I sped through any cleaning duties so that I could hang out with the others upstairs. One of them had the colour of my eye. Helen wore a plain white apron and did the frying most of the time, although sometimes she had to do serving duties with a tall Goth called Chris. She was easily a couple of years older than me, tall and slim, ordinary looking with a bleached hydrogen peroxide hairdo. The bottle job only served to heighten my infatuation, for I was in the middle of every teenager's wet dream, a full-blown Marilyn Monroe obsession. With a blotchy dye job, she was certainly no blonde bombshell. Even so, I didn't care. I might have been the young subterranean creature dressed in a funny looking coat that they kept out of sight in the basement, but I still managed to share a few precious moments wielding a wooden chip fork swirling chips round in a greasy polystyrene tray. Sometimes during quieter moments she'd add an inexplicable sense of mystery staring dejectedly out of the shop window. Starkly exposed, a life closed-off offering a tantalising vision to any unsuspecting passers-by, like someone out of a Hopper painting. Chris on the other hand couldn't stand still for more than five seconds. He danced as he moved in a continuous flow, and always with a fast rhythm. Pasty faced, well over six foot and pencil slim, he wore black and purple clothes the same colour as his crimped hair. Even though he worked in a chippy, he was dangerously disorganised. Most days he imitated the make-up and dress sense of his favourite bands; The Sisters of Mercy, Bauhaus and Berlin-era Bowie. His infectious enthusiasm blasting off about music always lifted any sorrow from our eyes and helped to transport me away from Helen's indifference.

FATHER DIAMOND

The fear and excitement of the furtive encounter at Falmer visited me often during the irregular rhythms of the daytime void. I had become mute. My lifestyle escape from all the guilt and shame was disappearing into a cool blue mist, fading out like the hooded dead. In order to banish the slow suicide taking over I decided to undertake a series of walks through the city. Reaching back into the past analogues of war where the traces of destruction might help to bring all the disparate parts together. I began locally, taking a shortcut through the mortal chill of St Pauls' churchyard, stopping almost immediately beside a gravestone elaborately decorated with a vivid assemblage of straw dolls, garden gnomes, teddy bears, plastic windmills and tinsel. At the exact same time, a few of the well-wrapped faithful lumbered toward the entrance doors of the 18th century English Italienate Baroque church. Swept up in the midst of hope's candle, I fell in behind the martyrs of the road and huddled in their back-of-centre pews for some minutes. The tatty paint-work, the flaking plaster, the grubby galleries which in daylight observed the Church of England's abject failure to engage with the local working class community, were mercifully obscured by shadow. In the dingy dark only the massed candles of the altar shone bright onto an image of Jesus. St Paul's late Father Diamond (who began his ministry back in 1969), quadrupled the size of the congregation during the eighties, providing a regular solace against the national catastrophe of Thatcherism. I discovered the late Father Diamond's legacy (he passed away in 1992) leafing through a booklet that I picked up just inside the front door. In the painting above the altar, Jesus looked down with compassion, his glowing heart wrapped in a crown of thorns and topped with a flaming cross. On either side stood the two witnesses, the Virgin Mary and the apostle John. I started to wonder what the most painted figure in western art really looked like. In the wake of the Second World War, Graham Sutherland described images of Christ's death as…'the most tragic of all themes, and yet inherent in it is the promise of salvation'. Many think they recognise him in a variety of different guises; the infant in Mary's arms, the wandering rabbi, the political prisoner, the crucified Saviour, or the kindly teacher and storyteller. For me, there was only one representation - Salvador Dali's consummate image depicting Christ hanging dolorously over the artist's hometown of Port Lligat in Spain. I think the fascination lies mainly in the dramatically exaggerated perspective of the crucified Christ, as we look down on him from the same parallel omnipotent angle that only 'God' the father would have understood. Notably, there is no attempt at a facial characterisation, which only adds to the wondrously eerie vision. During the Transubstantiation I got up, walked around the back of the pews, and looked up at the grandiose Baroque features just as the organ started moaning and the raging bells broke loose.

THE ROUNDABOUT

Increasingly, I viewed the world from the small balcony above the mini-roundabout directly outside the flat. I could even see it framed in the window if I craned forward when collapsed on the sofa. In the midst of a section of characterless grey tenements, it always appeared to be undergoing some form of re-construction. Outsourcing, another legacy of the growing privatisation begun under the Thatcher government, led to the council giving private contractors another expensive contract to carry out the works. With an army of white vans blocking parking spaces and causing traffic congestion, the constant grinding, banging, drilling, dust and vibration mixed with the monotonous fucking assault of Heart FM playing Peter Andre on repeat nearly finished me off. The occupation was not popular. Late one evening about a month after their arrival, as the night was darkening and a wild wind blew coldly, I started yelling at the roundabout, waving a salt container at it as though brandishing a sword.

"This is for the roundabout and the greedy ones that don't know how to give…"

"And this is for whoever made this heap of junk!"
Pshhhkkkkkkrrrrkakingkakingkakingtshchchchchchchchcch*ding*ding*ding …

The PC's days had been numbered for a while; AOL's dial-up handshake often petered out with a pathetic squawk. Exasperated, frustrated and fed up, I picked up the bulky yellowing CRT monitor, raised it above my head, and threw it over the balcony in the direction of the roundabout. Miraculously, it somehow lodged itself in a shopping trolley. More fodder for the

Prince of Darkness no doubt. Facing away from the balcony I threw out the salt container between my legs, like a 'Tweener' shot in tennis. It flew low and straight, hitting the centre of the roundabout in slow motion with a powder puff explosion.

Unknowingly, I had just invited the devil into my life...

In Leonardo's *The Last Supper*, Judas Iscariot knocks over a container of salt with his elbow. The scene depicts the moment when Jesus announces that one of his disciples will betray him. A ghost-like brown blob accidentally overturned, spilling its contents onto the table. An idea believed to be originated by Leonardo that has allowed Christians to assume a connection between the spilling of salt and the crucifixion of Christ. I spent another half an hour staring at the crystals 'snowing down' on the roundabout, happily oblivious to the fallen saltshaker omen, even though some researchers believe it may suggest rehabilitation instead.

FUCK POLITICS

I remembered walking the entire length of the Holloway Road from Highbury Corner to Archway, stopping roughly halfway at The Coronet. A former Picture Palace designed with a Modern Art Deco feel, it had been subjected to full Spoonification in the mid 90s. The boozy ferry was full of silent afternooners, nursing their pints like dead men in the midst of life. Passing through the Brick Lane area, I took a photo of an iconic spray job depicting a few lines from Scorsese's sombre masterpiece *Taxi Driver*. The image fused Roy Lichtenstein's 1963

Hopeless painting with Travis Bickle's infamous 'Someday a real rain will come' quote. Employing the same luminous colours as the pop art pioneer's original, the teary-eyed young woman had bright red lips and yellow hair flowing in glamorous curls. Sad girls, women in distress, the struggle beneath the glamour, merging 'low-brow' comic style aesthetics with the 'high-brow' themes of old master paintings. Melodramatic in the extreme, Lichtenstein's art always had a very immediate and of-the-moment feel that would soon vanish, just like the Sclater Street spray job. Only a few weeks later it changed from full colour into a pale ghost-like version. I stood for a moment longer thinking about imitation dispatches from a pure pop world. Born out of Pop's artistic tendencies, Basquiat and Keith Haring took graffiti from the street into mainstream galleries, Basquiat eventually becoming the darling of corporate America. Perhaps he was trying to subvert from within, when all the racism and class inequality that featured so heavily in his work ended up being assimilated onto trainers, t-shirts, caps and Tote bags.

'They all sign up in the end one way or another', I repeated the haunting world vision of Jarman's media mogul, Borgia Ginz to myself heading off down the south side of Sclater Street adjacent to the railway lines. On the way back I stopped at my favourite corner shop run by a bunch of Turkish guys just off Deptford Broadway. Their English hadn't advanced much beyond the 'cheers' or 'thank you' stages yet, but they always smiled and seemed polite. Taking the longer route via the new steel bridge on Ha'Penny Hatch, I passed a red swastika alongside the words *Fuck Politics* sprayed in free-hand like a tag.

SEXUAL POETICS

"It's only a tenner in Shagaluf; they're desperate and go after older men all the time."

The conversation on the table opposite took an about turn.

"Ten quid for a blow-job?"

Magaluf, a fiction in itself, 500 metres of shame 'Made in the UK, Destroyed in Magaluf', or so the t-shirts say. I finished up the last dregs of my Americano and thought about all the horrifying newspaper photos denigrating mostly women. Back in the late 60s, Magaluf was still uncommercialised and beautiful like the Bahamas. But then at the height of the package boom in the 70s, the Balearic Islands attracted over two million Brits a year, with nearly half of them staying in one-star knocking shops. I remembered when my mum and dad managed to scrape enough cash together for us to go to Cala D'Or in the early 80s. One of many small bays that attracted tourists, it was mainly populated by well-to-do middle-class types with bars, restaurants and hotels run by ex-pat alkies. My old man was not so keen on going abroad and had to be talked round. It didn't take long before the sun and sangria changed his mind. That and regular games on Miguel's Crazy Golf course, where the prizes convert Bravo bull figures made out of injected PVC and plastic flamenco dolls with red dresses trimmed with black lace.

Another round of squally downpours let rip behind the café. God knows why I'd come out on the bike. At least the wind would be with me on the long drag back down Tooley Steet and Jamaica Road. I still needed to go to a supermarket for a tube of toothpaste, a loaf and some soup. Flicking a few stray crumbs off the table, I stood up and glanced at the menu board from the restaurant next door. Chicken Ballotine? Never heard of it... Did remind me of a guy back in school, Mark Ballantyne I think he was called. He embarrassed the English teacher real bad reading aloud an extract from *Lord of the Flies*. It was near the bit about Simon's nose bleed in Chapter Nine when Ballantyne ad-libbed in perfect monotone, 'Miss, I can see your tits!'

We all roared about while the poor teacher could merely look down at her wide open blouse. The colour of her blush matched only by the vast pink nudes in our adolescent dreaming.

TAPIOCA DE WANKEUR

The long walks began to bring their own distinctness to that time. They took me away from countless moments gazing emptily from my bedroom window or the balcony, seeking either the terrible beauty of the roundabout or the tragic comedy of the Chicken Lady. Struggling to sleep with the days going on and on without end, the pair of them provided a sense of relief from many moments spent cooped up inside.

Taking refuge on a bench in Hyde Park one hot afternoon in July, a tranquil breeze brought a certain uplifting spirit. Nearby, grey squirrels hugged the plane trees and patrolled bins by the coffee stands, while reed warblers, robins and blackbirds provided a silvery, crystal soundtrack. Exuberant kids danced and screamed on their way to meet Peter Pan, evoking pleasant childhood memories of my first visit to London. Thankfully, the usual mob of disc heads chucking frisbees at each other had stayed away.

I was on my way to see Gilbert and George's *The Dirty Words Pictures* exhibition at the Serpentine. Outside Green Park tube station I'd picked up the Evening Standard. Inside the arts section an article asked the question, 'Are young British artists nincompoops and frauds?' In the interview, Brian Sewell and Matthew Collings debated the merits of modern British art. Sewell, that old dinosaur of art criticism never ceased to voice his disgust at the kind of conceptual art Gilbert and George served up. Ironically, another recent article from the same paper had focused on how George had saved 'key words' from Sewell's damning reviews of their work:

'Comely adolescent boy, black penis springing from white loins, youth with greasy torso, sodomolenos and tapioca de wankeur.'

I approached the impressive-looking Grade II-listed building, (formerly known as The Magazine), just southwest of the Serpentine from Kensington Gardens. Folded like a piece of origami, Daniel Libeskind's angular metal pavilion, a masterpiece of flat-pack design glinted in the low sunshine. Put up in less than 20 days, it had been made from sheets of aluminium riveted together to create a continuous form. *Eighteen Turns* I learnt that it had been called from the blurb next to the gallery entrance, a reference to how it seemingly folded over itself.

It was getting close to 5pm when I approached the reception desk. The gallery assistant had a long thin face with bright and young eyes. She spoke with a matter-of-fact voice folding a piece of paper into three strips at the same time.

"I didn't realise you needed to book a ticket. Are

there any slots left?"

"Should be OK, you might have to wait a few moments before I can let you through. We close at 6pm, so it's the last timed entry. If you wait near the shop I'll call out as soon as it's clear to enter."

I hung around reception leafing through one of the large format 64 page exhibition catalogues heavily illustrated with the 26 photograph-pictures from the show. Introductions by curator Lisa G. Corrin and Michael Bracewell discussed how the artists had recorded the traces of melancholy within easy reach of their fine Georgian town house on Fournier Street. I'd passed their place (just off Brick Lane) on another recent outing through the heart of Spitalfields, close to Nicholas Hawksmoor's glorious Baroque Christ Church. The works were set against the backdrop of the Silver Jubilee in 1977, when England (or more specifically the East End) was not a particularly pretty sight. Back then the urban landscape appeared to be dominated by drunks, the homeless and the re-emergence of the National Front, (where the violence of skinhead culture became interlinked with football hooliganism). The images also contained a multiplicity of ethnic minorities, office workers and soldiers. England was memorably described by George as, 'a big pile of shit with a punk rocker waving a swastika on top of it'. I couldn't wait to go in…Drifting through the first of four interconnected galleries, I found myself surrounded by photographic images mounted in thin, black aluminium frames, arranged in grids, behind Perspex. They were all hung snugly up against each other and low to the polished floor on pristine, whiter-than-white walls. The artists had placed most of the graffiti, from which the titles were derived, at the top of the works...

> *Prick Ass   Cunt Scum   Prostitute Poof*
> *Bollocks We're All Angry*

The sleek presentation of the show contrasted perfectly with a disturbingly bleak set of pictures, documenting ritual poses surrounded by the city, assembling the endemic aggression using a heraldic mixture of swear words, eroticism, and images of power and religion. I could never quite tell whether their old fashioned English duplicity (even though Gilbert is blatantly Italian) was being exploitative; snooping on the so-called low life elements of society. Recording images of the underbelly for middle class journalists and pricks like myself to brand the alleged images of racism, racist...There was no one about when I returned to the reception area, the desk had been left unoccupied and the shop cordoned off. Light greeted me as I stepped outside onto the dusty path, past a scuffling blackbird as I walked towards the Albert Memorial and back into the throng of more familiar solitudes.

A couple of weeks later, I ended up in more or less the same spot on Chester Street where Gilbert and George had documented most of the graffiti back in '77. Stopping at a large expanse of brick wall to take photos of tiny left-overs, including a stencilled tribute to Banksy's George W. Bush and Saddam (in the form of an intimate embrace), next to a curious tagline, *Fuck the Poshpunks*. I crossed over the same bridge subjected to a litany of racist slogans back in the 70s, some of them featured on the cover of a book I purchased from the Brick Lane Bookshop titled; *Auschwitz and East London*. Connecting across space and time the graffiti at Ha'Penny Hatch to the echo of punk's flirtation with swastikas, the ultimate emblem for annoying the establishment. On all these paths, fetishised images of Nazism and the Holocaust only resulted in the nihilism of *Belsen was a Gas,* Jon Savage's 'one-line, very sick joke.' Around Hoxton Square, I passed a couple of ghetto rebels with lumberjack beards sitting on a bench, hands in pockets, wearing low-slung washed out 501s. Visualising the dots and loops of a new Bitches Brew, a pair of scooters set to stun…

"Will we need to prepare for the sessions?"

"Dunno…I went to his house several times, had about 10 tunes for him. He chose a few and then made sketches of the rest."

"But I only have a snare drum and a cymbal. I thought we would just rehearse that one track."

"Don't worry; he was really cool with me; full of encouragement. Spoke about things like hearing the collective. Besides, nobody else has heard 'em before."

GENERATION X

Inevitably, like water far down a well, the little bit of money I'd eked out after leaving the record company started to run dry. The glum indifference of never opening the door and waking up in the middle of the day with nothing to do was increasingly aided by a vibrating soundless hum. Kafka's 'decent into the cold abyss of oneself' meant that my lifestyle escape literally wasn't working. If ever anyone did knock on the door, I would simply lie down flat on the carpet and hide behind the sofa. Any phone calls were screened while I piloted a tiny spaceship through a monochrome field of alien nasties, blasting any unsuspecting victims clean out of the sky. I kept the blinds drawn; the windows closed and ate tins of bland tasting soup day-in day-out. I didn't understand what was happening. It must have been very complicated. I didn't like it or want it, but *it* was just there. On days when I could let go of it, I felt much better. Mostly, I couldn't discuss it with anyone. What I desperately needed was to offer my forgiveness, to be able to just say something, anything. Whenever I did venture out for shopping it was usually at night and only to stores with the new self-checkouts. Sometimes I stared at BBC News for hours watching the *War on Terror* unfold with the sound on mute. When the last of the Temazepam ran out nothing was left but the slow fade into dreams. Moving from side-to-side, my legs ached from all the walking, while I burned for the new life of death. Increasingly connected to the world in momentary fragments, only Coupland's *Generation X* offered the tricks to elimination, the totally unreal reality of existence. 'Dead at 30, Buried at 70.' Like a headless corpse exhaling a final sigh, I stumbled around in neon groves abandoning myself to the soul kitchen. Could I ever learn to forget? Block out all the guilt and shame. Now I inhabited a dingy estate on a depressive's diet of downers amid total withdrawal from the corporate drones. During sleepless nights while the darkness settled and my homeless ghost transformed itself into a coffin shape, too afraid to look back at the ruined towers of fragile loneliness. Days became like Dag's silent drift. Ambling around hollowly acting out life's motions, reaching the crisis point where the shadow of youth is erased forever.

    I decided it was time to hunker down and revert to type. If I could not look my own history in the eye then I would have to seek comfort elsewhere. Seeing as I struggled to get off the couch most days I turned to the Victorian day-bed theories of Freud, in particular, *Mourning and Melancholia*, an essay written in the wake of the Great War. Almost immediately, I dipped my toes into an arcane language where the dead occupy a place in our bodies.

Haunting us in mourning which doesn't develop naturally, in mourning that goes wrong...There is no true internalisation...The dead are taken into us but don't become part of us...They just occupy a particular place in our bodies. But in melancholia, the pain of loss is felt within the unconscious…

Not surprisingly, the miraculous dawn didn't occur, and I later discovered the father of psychoanalysis had been debunked as a charlatan in 1975 by Nobel prize-winning scientist, Peter Medawar, who called his theories, 'the most stupendous intellectual confidence trick of the 20th century.'

I began to cough and touch my ribs at the same time.

"Well, anyway, here I am. Will everything be awful forever?"

Outside the rain fell steadily against the roundabout, the balcony, the road, the pavement, and the ghosts of South East London's past, present and future on the estates out-house walling. There in Freud's eyes, an interminable reminder of the burning flesh of men.

'So, how does this make you feel? Well, I really think you should quit smoking.'

Air's dark, ambling mechanical larynx, sought the real connection of being held in the mind of another. A robot whispers human and computer-generated dialog. I will drive on that road forever...

THE WORLD AT WAR

'The day the soldiers came the people were gathered together. The men were taken to garages and barns. The women and children were driven into a church. Here, they heard the firing as their men were shot. Then, they were killed too...'

Aerial shots of the massacre at Oradour-sur-Glane combined with the elegiac tones of Sir Laurence Olivier, which grace Thames Television's landmark series *The World at War*. I'd borrowed the new 10 disc special collector's edition during a rare sortie to the library opposite the estate just off Deptford High Street. The widescreen epic *The Battle of the Bulge* provided the inspiration after another outing on Channel Five. Most of the 26 episodes on the box-set turned out to be about an hour long. Despite such a tragic subject matter (or perhaps because of it), I always found them absorbing after hitting the play button. Even though I'd had issues with the great man himself, Laurence Olivier, who had described my old teenage hearthrob as an 'utter bitch' on the UK production of *The Prince and the Showgirl*. Yet before the shoot, at a joint press conference held in New York, Marilyn had famously called her co-star 'a dreamboat' and said England sounded 'adorable.' At that stage Olivier was so enraptured by her that he worried he might fall in love. In the end, he livened up the drab post-war headlines with the outspoken attack. I couldn't argue with his mellifluous delivery throughout the *World at War* series though, which stylishly shaped and nurtured what Vonnegut infamously referred to as, 'the world's biggest suicide note.'

"Anyone home?"

My flat mate caught me by surprise bundling in from nowhere, carrying a rucksack and grasping a handful of mail at the same time.

"In the lounge, I'd forgotten you lived here! Where was it you went to again?"

"Just nip to the loo first."

I grabbed the remote and pressed pause, swirling the dregs in a coffee cup with a fragile handle. Carefully, I pulled out a piece of paper from a pocket in my joggers and noticed how the light shone through it.

"Smells like a compost heap in here. I'll open a window."

"Sorry, I know it gets quite musty sometimes. How was - "

"Poland. Sure I told you before we left. We flew in to Warsaw, took the train to Krakow before heading north to Christophe's place in Toruń. Not a million miles from the German border. James was so funny; he went to get a haircut straight after landing."

"That's a tradition for him though isn't it?"

My flatmate smiled and sat down in the armchair ripping open a couple of Lovefilm envelopes containing the latest movie fix.

"Managed to keep everyone awake at the hostels we stayed at too. My God he can snore like a trooper!"

"Bet you were popular!"

"Thankfully, no one knew who it was. Otherwise we'd have been lynched! And he snored on all the trains too! What's this you're watching?"

"*The World at War.* It's a new box set I got out from the library."

"Jesus, feels like I've just come back from the bloody Second World War. I'll leave you to it then, my Dougie Sirk films have arrived now anyway!"

"Which ones?"

"*All That Heaven Allows* and *Written on the Wind.* You know how I love a good melodrama…"

I pressed the play button again…From Blitzkrieg to Operation Barbarossa to the beaches of Dunkirk and the relentless pounding at El Alemain, the episodes kept coming. Like a bank of waves lined up, one behind the other, while I teetered on the edge of the blackest void, awaking to the sounds of air raid sirens, a head full of the disasters of war. I was losing my own battle with the fine art of forgetting. No matter how painful it was to digest, the powerful reminders of the inhumane consequences of warfare, like Goya's 19th century series of etchings, remained like any other unheeded warning from history.

SPACE DEMENTIA

"Hey, are you in there? Come on man, open up…it's me, Maestro! Got a little something for ya!"

Maestro had the unique honour of being the first person to knock at the front door for months. I couldn't hide because sitting opposite; my flatmate was busy flicking through the photos from a large hardback titled *100 SUNS*. I'd noticed some of the spectacular images in the book on a special WWII display at the library. As you might expect, there were exactly one hundred photographs to mark the United States' atmospheric and underwater nuclear tests (conducted between July 1945 and November 1962). On the cover blurb, Oppenheimer's infamous 'I am become Death' quote after the Trinity test in New Mexico, served as a potent reminder of the profound questions confronting the Manhattan Project scientists ...

A fellow traveller from Uncle Rupert's shallow money trench, Maestro's erudite vibrations always maintained a special place. Especially whenever I thought of his desk, a wasteland of broken images, where, according to him, the rats in the alley lost their bones. He always used to quip, 'I could have a side-line, From Junk to Jesus!'

It was Maestro who supplied the office with weekly doses of mind-numbing toxins, dropping small packets into hungry drawers, like a secret Santa bearing gifts all year round. As a result, the hotsteppers he worked for were completely trashed most of the time. You knew they were on one when the bass blasted across their little corner of downstairs, pumping out heavy vibes, nothing but dub and happiness. With Maestro in control of all the madness it was a miracle that they ever got anything done. Drop by to drop out. Chemical days, raw beats, and pure rushing with every build, the krew consisted of a rude collection of mash-ups who stared with eyes closed.

One of the most memorable stories that did the rounds recalled when Maestro phoned for a courier late one night. Worse than usual, after another long day on the green monophonics, naturally he felt the sting and sunk into a minor coma across the reception desk somehow holding on to the package he'd arranged to be collected. The courier eventually turned up and buzzed for the best part of 10 minutes, with no answer. Apparently, it took someone from a hush-hush meeting in the crow's nest to come down and check out what was going on. Initially they found the reception area deathly silent, with only the noise of the wind under the door. Unbelievably, they must have walked straight past this ghostly Buddha of Suburbia, statuesque behind the desk. Evidently, Maestro didn't seem to be breathing at all. The funniest thing was that he held onto the package throughout, and even when they let the courier in neither could wrestle it off him.

Maestro wore dark sunglasses, a tan coloured Mos Def & Talib Kweli "Black Star" t-shirt, with big, flared up blue jeans that swept the ground to gather blessings and the deepest confessions.

"Nice one bro, I was beginning to think you might have moved away."

"Not yet, soon maybe. Like the t-shirt. Is that a new album?"

"Nah man…it's a few years old now. They got the title from The Right Excellent Marcus Garvey. You don't buy a life; you live a life. It's a reference to the shipping line he founded after the First World War. Forever blessed by the spirit, the Right One supposedly declared himself Provisional President of Africa. I studied him and the Black Star Line a bit at Uni. They had some good quality frequencies in commercial trade and fraternities' back then man."

We moved through the hallway to the lounge where I introduced him to my flatmate. He was feverishly highlighting things to do in the Guardian Guide.

"Yeah that Garvey, he was quite a character. Got

arrested and charged for mail fraud and for advertising the sale of stocks in a ship."

"Really, when was all this?"

"Early 1920s I think, he made bail for a couple of thousand dollars, but a small number of the stock owners wanted to pursue the matter further. In the name of wealth the soul is always hard for the dollar bill man. So Garvey spoke out against rival African-American groups, accusing them of a conspiracy to get him imprisoned. Then the mainstream press got hold of it, and presented him as a con artist who swindled the African-American people!"

"America is so fucked up!" I inhaled a little, while my flatmate looked on uninterested.

"When it did eventually go to court after a number of postponements, the old country folks fined him and sent him down for five years, while his three co-defendants got off scot free!"

"Five years?"

"Yeah man, so he looks at the judge and district attorney and starts shouting abuse in the courtroom, calling them - damned dirty Jews!"

Maestro took off his sunglasses felt around in his jeans and carefully lifted out a whopping five skinner. After sniffing the green leaves quietly to himself he lit up and put his shades back on. Almost immediately, my flatmate left the room.

"Is he OK? Seems a bit uptight."

"He's fine, just a bit tired I guess. He's hardly ever here and besides, he only got back from travelling round Poland the other day."

"Poland? That is a trip. Stalinists and political dreamers, I've heard they're still steeped in World War

Two. Sure I read somewhere Poland was the only one of the allies not present in the Victory parade – hard to get your head round man!"

"I've been watching loads of the actual war footage on a new box set I just borrowed from the library."

Maestro inhaled a massive toke and held his breath for a few moments. "This shit is still beating strong in the target man, nice…"

"You know the Polish people tried so hard but literally everyone let them down. I think my flatmate might have had his photos of Auschwitz developed. I could see if he's got them if you're interested?"

I looked at him, trying to gauge a reaction. It was impossible to tell anything with those dark shades on.

"Very, very heavy subject matter man, guess I should, but right now, I'm not so sure."

There were nearly 40 photos in a royal blue Jessops pouch emblazoned with the tagline, 'Bringing Your Memories to Life.' Sized 7" x 5" they had been developed in black and white, and already looked like they were fading into a distant past. After leafing through the set at a fair pace, Maestro passed over all but one of the images. If the ruins, reconstruction, railway ramps and barbed wire fences weren't enough, the sheer scale of camp II (Birkenau and its subsidiaries) literally took our breath away. I realised he had stopped toking as he sat back in the chair holding onto the photo of a memorial stone.

"A cry of despair and a warning to humanity – wow man!"

As my flatmate poked his head in the lounge, Maestro looked up and shook his head. "Why did you take them?"

Still clinging to the door, he replied slowly at first, "I don't really know. A record I suppose. I mean you could say Auschwitz is the ultimate site of memory. Besides, we tried to be respectful at all times. You wouldn't believe how some groups posed in front of the main gates and..."

Even though he still hadn't entered the room fully, he paused to take a gulp, "the crematoriums!"

"Jesus! What is wrong with some people?" I quickly put the photos down on the floor.

"In Krakow, we found the DEF enamel factory where they filmed *Schindler's List*. It was a little bit out of town over a bridge. About half-way up the stairs leading to Schindler's office there was a small semi-circular room with a lone candle and book to sign in and add thoughts. Silent and peaceful, we had the entire place to ourselves. There were framed stills from the film on the walls too, almost like a mini-storyboard. At least they hadn't gone too over the top with it all mind."

"I'm still not sure why anyone would want to take this type of photo though man. I mean how can you possibly justify it? Yes, for educational purposes, in order to help out a fellow brother. But *posing* in a place where such immeasurable suffering went down, what does that kind of shit say about us or life even?"

"That most of us are either very, very foolish or completely cretinous or both. Probably both!"

"Not to mention sick, and shallow, and thoughtless and self-centred. It pollutes the air man. Especially if you think about all the crap going down in America, Iraq and Afghanistan right now."

"From Krakow we could only buy a one way ticket to Auschwitz!"

"No!"

"We thought it must have been a wind up. The classic lost in translation vibe. But that's all they would sell us. Hopefully it'll get sorted soon. Not only that, we arrived early, way too early in fact. So early, we had to wait in the café before the museum opened. A contingent of about 40 or so was sat at most of the tables and chairs. I don't remember where they were all from. Most were already tucking into the breakfast menu like no tomorrow. My stomach still churns at the thought of it."

After that there was a pause until my flatmate finally entered the lounge and gathered up the photos before beating a hasty retreat to the cinema.

Maestro stood up and moved toward the balcony, just as I felt an odd sensation in my gut like a car juddering to a halt.

"For some reason those photos remind me of a book I read recently, *Cat's Cradle* by Kurt Vonnegut. Do you know it?"

"No, but I have read *Slaughterhouse Five*."

"*Cat's Cradle* is about the fears of realising Armageddon. He wrote it in 1963 just after the Cuban missile crisis. It's the story of one man's desire to collect material for a book to be called 'The Day the World Ended', featuring accounts of what so-called important Americans had done on the day the first atomic bomb was dropped on Hiroshima. In the book Vonnegut created a new religion, 'Bokononism'. The holy scripture of Bokononism was the ever-growing 'Books of Bokonon', written by Bokonon (a British Episcopalian Negro from the island of Tobago, real name Lionel Boyd Johnson), as a way to distract the people of San Lorenzo from their pitiful lives. And you know what was sacred to Bokononists? Not God; just one thing: man!"

"Guess a religion doesn't have to be true to be useful."

"Exactly! Vonnegut cleverly used the island of San Lorenzo to portray how lies can help mankind more than truth. Anyway look man, I'm going to head off now and leave you to your meditation and elimination."

Maestro lit up the five-skinner and took three quick pulls, inhaling with a deep hissing sound. Unless a strange quirk of fate threw us together again, I knew this would be the last time for us in this place.

WI-FI EVANGELISM

After the episode with the salt container, I learnt a useful tip from my neighbour! He said if you hung around for long enough outside the Methodist Church at the top of the High Street, you got a strong Wi-Fi signal. I'd no idea how he found this out, but the old 'cosy corner' drop-in soon became a regular haunt. Once, close by the cold and dark triangular shaped bit behind the red-bricked mission, I heard voices screeching as though in hunger. In the circling gloom, I could only make out their silhouettes at first. One hairy and rough looking, the other small and bony.

"Where d'you think you're going? Come here you little."

"Leave me alone. You don't understand, I'm not your slave."

They pushed each other forward into the spark of a street lamp. Suddenly, I could see a face swelled with a malevolent aquatic spirit. Strong and blunt, a hammer shaped fist grabbed a pony tail while arms and legs kicked and flapped like a trapped bird. From its neck, the hairy creature then unexpectedly pulled out a fixed blade. Their nebulous shapes fell back into the murky corner, a murderous dance crawling toward the refuse of humanity. With all the might of decayed ambition, a set of bared teeth bit down hard into a longhaired limb, before kicking and rolling over onto its back, smiling with cancelled eyes, a face all covered with blood. I glimpsed a hoof placed on top of a shoulder blade and a shudder ran the length of my back…

SINNER

Occasionally on the opposite side of the roundabout to where the Chicken Lady rushed about in agitation stood Sinner. A plump middle aged woman, with a toothless, round red face. Her mushroomed shaped dark hair sometimes had the odd leaf sticking out of it. I often watched her pushing a trolley full of stuff over the pedestrian crossing to the exact same spot beneath the balcony. The Myth of Sisyphus on the invisible streets of South East London. With the morning sunrise a recurring ritual took place, as she pushed her heavy cart into position until she found the strength to do it all over again. Whatever the weather, she wore a light grey sweatshirt with similar coloured jogging bottoms under a long dark blue puffer jacket. I noticed she never took any clothing off on warmer days, even when sweating profusely. Mostly, she remained static on the pavement, resolute and silent. The fear and echoes of the abyss protected by a bulletproof Bible in her hip pocket. On days when the Chicken

Lady patrolled the environs nearby, she spewed out lengthy streams of consciousness from one side of her mouth. An incoherent jumble of religious symbolism delivered with flared nostrils. A modern day Lucky tangled in a web of clichés. It was curious how the awkward strutting and constant shadow of the Chicken Lady set her off. One hazy afternoon, as shadows engulfed the estate, I decided to see if I could spark my own volley of verbal chaos. I headed downstairs toward the door entry on tenterhooks, hoping the usual shufflers were occupied elsewhere. Thankfully, the coast was clear as I rounded the corner by the "Love Over Gold" mural. Facing the roundabout, I saw Sinner nestled in position. An endgame like 'a speck in the void.'

I ambled slowly into the wide grey world and stopped a yard in front of her red face. I settled on her green eyes, calm and cold behind nickel-rimmed spectacles. She paused muttering to herself for a few seconds until the roundabout was clear.

"And the proper moisture for the land is the dew, all this is all, I mean the land has become so polluted and stagnant that's why the righteous will come for the washing of the land, and by rights they'll make everything good."

I gave a small cough, "Right."

"And it's supposed to be the dew; the dew is the moisture for the land."

With that she stopped while a car passed by. I could see the sweat running down her cheeks. I waited patiently with rigid muscles, expecting her to start again at any moment. Finally, after a tense minute or so, she shrugged and moved behind her trolley in a gesture of defiance. By now a heavy drizzle had started to fall. The sound of a skidding car provided a distraction for another few seconds. When I turned round again she was pointing straight at me.

"Demons, demons, demons and er…the devil and birthright. It's all to do with their birthright."

RHYTHMIC GRACE

As the old man's condition began to worsen, mother claimed she wanted to top herself. She hated her life and had nothing to live for. You couldn't really blame her, most days she hardly got anything out of him. All day slumped in the one chair like a cud chewing cow, grinding his falsies with a rhythmic grace. Heavy eyelids gazing nowhere, from dream to dream and mumbling like a fool in a futile struggle. Only loo breaks and a painful shuffle to the kitchen at dinnertime provided any respite. I sympathised with her, especially during my own long evenings spent staring into the dying fires from the balcony's edge. The last time down at their place I found a couple of small notepads by the phone. They showed some of his jottings before shit got really bad…

WIFE WENT DOWN FOR BLOOD
TEST & FLU JAB
NURSE SAID THAT SHE
WOULD
COME ROUND & GIVE
ME MY FLU JAB AT
HOME BECCAUSE I CAN'T
WALLK VERY WELL &
HAVEN'T YET – SHE HASN'T

BEEN YET?
NOT BEEN YET…
BLOOD TEST!

<u>DO NOT TOUCH:</u>
Chelsey
0800 083 2726
NUISANCE ~~PROSPECT~~
              PROSPECT £33

£20 NOTES
TO BE OK

MUM TO TAKE
2' 00 THIS
AFTERNOON

RE 132 JH TOENAIL SOFTENER
£7.15
Enclosed is the softener
To soften Tough toe nails
Before trimming @ a cost
of £7.15

THE BALLAD OF
DOROTHY PARKER

    The time had come to begin the purges proper. I gathered up a load of CD's that I'd blagged from various record companies, bundled them into a trolley and headed for the Sense charity shop on the High Street. After emptying out an assortment of albums and singles onto a desk in their cramped back room, I began to search idly through a hotchpotch of paperbacks, until I came upon a relatively new copy of *The Collected Dorothy Parker*. After I bought it and returned to the late evening/early morning apocalypse which loomed large, having been firmly re-established of late. As expected, it hadn't taken long for Lazarus to shake it loose. So much so, the Council asked if we could keep another record of all the disturbances. The Sci-fi Messiah must have gotten wise to us though, silencing his radio just before 11pm and then notching it up again after 3 am - the exact same hours as the Council's 'noisy neighbour' call-out service. I kept tabs for about a week or so: Friday 29th & Saturday 30th Sept, Sunday 1st October (noise started at 4am!), Monday 2nd, Sunday 8th October (both nights - called Council, no answer).

Seeking a new oblivion, I managed to blag another batch of jellies from the Docs, which negated everything so effectively, it felt like a time lapse had helped me move out of my own body for good. Night after night, I drifted into an eroded swamp of dreams, pursued by ghosts circling in the dark of midnight. Among swirling waves of mad fantasy that longed to escape, a secret rhythm penetrated my unconscious and drew out a succession of imaginings. Waiting for night to fall with the wisecracking Dorothy Parker, until the pills took hold and made my eyes drift from the page. Here and there, I fell painlessly into a succession of dreams...

It might have been afternoon and I was walking above the Undercliff on the chalky tops. A discoloured dirty and greying teddy bear, with one eye torn off and a slightly skewwhiff back leg held my attention. In the distance, on track to either rescue or pass by, the sound of a ship's horn lost at sea called to the coast. An old lady dressed in a threadbare overcoat and a faded lime green headscarf appeared from nowhere. A pair of chapped lips struck up a familiar piece of propaganda…

'Hitler has only got one ball; the other is in the Albert Hall.'

I looked out to a sea infused by passages of grey and black with touches of white, green and brown. The surface danced with a light golden colour and reflected a solitary moonbeam. It grew bigger by the second, until a dark echo ate up the rocks and boulders that surrounded the battlements. On a wooden bench next to a toilet block I sat engulfed by a warm tingle, before everything plunged into the deepest vortex, falling faster and faster as one by one my limbs detached. With the warmth of letting go, the bare abstraction of nothingness melted into the hazy water leaving only plaintive cries creeping out across the moonlight.

A new vision flashed across me and I was surrounded by a group of teenagers. They were waiting for someone to take a white three wheeler for a spin. At dusk, an open invitation on the forecourt, its low build and recumbent driving position took everyone by surprise. Florid and flamboyant, I got in and pedalled it through the town centre until our Bacchanalian Dithyramb reached the train station. I hung back by the entrance gates while the gang distracted the guard at the ticket office. Then we sped through the barrier. Embracing our moment of triumph, we carried the booty up the steps in full view of everyone on the platform.

"Begone!" the chorus shouted waving goodbye to Sir Clive's Doodle-buggy as it disappeared on the first train south.

Laughter cut in above the sound of the floorboards vibrating, acting in the same way as a drumhead imparting its energy and motion to the air on the other side of the room. I listened hesitantly for an instant, then turned over and dozed some more.

This time, I dreamt I was walking through my parent's house listening to the Prince track "The Ballad of Dorothy Parker". The drum loop had an underwater quality, like a thumping beneath the underside of a boat, while the synths ricocheted as though rebounding off sheet metal. I heard another sound from somewhere else that I couldn't quite make out. Then, at the end of the hallway I came to a new room that I hadn't seen before. I pushed open a door coloured peach and black into a freshly-built home studio. A dark haired woman wearing black clothes and thick rimmed specs was testing the audio wiring of a brand new console.

"Let's record!"

A lone voice spoke through the control room monitors and began to play a discordant run of jazz chords on a beaten up Wurlitzer. The engineer stopped checking the wiring and started recording. Impatient to get the idea down, the pair of them worked fast and quietly, almost in silence. It didn't take long before they'd finished all the overdubs and the musician joined the engineer to listen to the playback. But something was wrong with the recording.

"It sounds flat, what's going on? There's no high-end!"

Worried that the musician would be angry, the engineer plugged in a set of headphones, turned up the monitor level and started fiddling with all the faders and pots. Then she got the voltmeter out and noticed that one half of the power supply rails were down. The console had only been recording at half power - not enough to record any treble.

"Sounds kinda dull, doesn't it?"

"Fits the song perfectly though, I like it!"

The musician tapped his feet and nodded along to the dreamy vibes.

"It's the sound of music falling apart, fucking up left, right and centre. It's dirty and in need of repair."

Slumped on a sofa in the control room, my breathing became heavy and I started sweating and feeling woozy. I got up and hurried out of the room, running until all my escape routes were closed off. Now I was in a different house going from one room to another, through a succession of empty corridors and cold passageways. Eventually I came to a tiny room bathed in a symphony of complimentary colours. There amongst pale lilac walls, a broken red and green tiled floor, chrome yellow chairs and a bed sprinkled with light green-citron pillows and sheets, I glimpsed the deathly silent image of a blanket stained blood red. Immediately, an intense horror came over me like a thunderbolt gathered in my heart.

From a window far off, I watched two figures on a driveway enclosed by a canopy of beech and silver birch, their shadows exiled on the concrete. They were approaching a Georgian door painted cerulean blue in a fanlight frame. The building was set back from a busy main road while the pavement was littered with discarded leaflets. A woman on reception greeted the pair with a continuous smile.

That day in the King and Queen when you disappeared for nearly half an hour. Fuck! How could a faint line assume an air of unreality and suddenly change spring to winter.

"If you'd rather not talk about it then that's fine, I'm always here for you."

I heard a voice say to a small, pale and pitiful figure lying in a great big bed.

By now I had positioned myself behind a two-way mirror. My side was much darker, with very little light reflected back allowing more light from the other side to pass through. Like an observation tool for wounded animals, I suddenly felt like a surveillance officer or zoo keeper. The mirror was made out of a large, shatterproof acrylic sheet, perfect for the safety of animals or families of concern.

The childlike woman in the great big bed didn't speak. The other, supposedly an old friend, kept on talking and nagging her the whole time. Continually, she asked the pale woman to explain herself, while assuring her that she wouldn't say a thing to anyone. As she continued blithely on the small woman began to cry.

"Have you got a cold? Oh you poor thing, here, take my handkerchief. Oh never mind, I see you've already got a pink chiffon one on the go. You really ought to get a box of tissues lying here all alone and upset with no-one around."

The pale woman seemed to be holding back something from the speaker, who carried on regardless, chastising her for living in a little furnished apartment, with no belongings, no roots, nothing in fact.

"Why don't you forget all about that horrible whatshisname and try to meet someone else, someone kind and considerate that you can get married to and have your own place, with a nice couple of kids in tow eh? Instead of your horrible little life just drifting along and falling away from the world, you know it's not right for a woman like you."

Holding out her right hand, the pale woman just blew her nose and asked the speaker for a spare handkerchief.

PART TWO

| The Lake District |

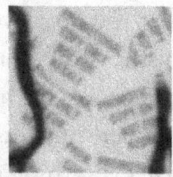

I'M DOING JASON!

"This is a story about a woman who owned a precious pen. Nothing particularly special or expensive even, but nonetheless unique to her. She always carried it around wherever she went, scribbling little bits of nonsense into an old notebook, making out lists on scraps of paper or bus tickets, not forgetting all those attempts at completing the daily crossword. She enjoyed thinking up little sayings and observations for friends or relatives that would later be put into birthday cards or the like. The pen wrote nicely and didn't use too much ink.

She woke up late one morning and felt a bit groggy. Dashing down both sets of the communal stairs, her jacket caught on the handlebars of a bike left at the bottom of the hallway. She wriggled free only to stumble into a pile of cassettes meant for next door's video shop. They had been mistakenly pushed through her letterbox. Kicking them aside, she prised open the door and glanced at her watch. Pegging it across the road, she could still make it into work at a respectable hour if she caught the next bus. Just as she was approaching the bus stop the heavens opened biblical style. The sheer ferocity of the downpour forced everyone to run for shelter. She hadn't brought an umbrella with her, so she made straight for Costcutters and forced her way inside. Despite a train of drab folk huddled by the door, she managed to force a bit of space for herself next to the cash machine. She thought about finishing the crossword from yesterday's paper while waiting for the monsoon to subside. Resting her bag on the ATM screen she began rummaging for the necessary items. She pulled out the paper straight away, folded in half on top of everything else, but after a good dig around couldn't find her special pen. It wasn't there. She cursed to herself. Where could it be? It was always in her bag. She bent down and started to look for it on the floor and even under the cash point. Her desperate search only served to annoy the others standing by the machine. She had to abandon it when the bus arrived and everyone made a mad dash outside. Eventually she followed them out and got on the bus last with a heavy heart, rueing the loss of her favourite thing in the world. She paid the driver with a crumpled fiver and went and sat at the back of the bus, shoulders slumped and wet through. As the double decker pulled away it kicked up a tumult of spray like a seaborne yellow mist. She took out a tissue and wiped a patch of condensation off the window for one long lasting look back at Costcutters.

    She continued to search her bag, emptying out the entire contents onto the seat opposite. Still it wasn't there. When she got home from work she looked for the pen in all the places she thought it might have been left. It was nowhere to be found. Later, after her flatmates returned from a night out she immediately grilled the pair of them, accusing them of borrowing it without asking. They both just shook their heads and insisted she was behaving irrationally. After a few more days of searching bags, checking rooms and drawers with further accusations of lies, she gave up and conceded that the pen must indeed be lost. In the hurly-burly theatre of sharing bricks and mortar with strangers, her special pen had become just another piece of collateral damage. The pain and frustration remained etched on her face for another couple of days until she could do without a pen no more. She took a bus to the local market and searched the stalls high and low for something nice and dependable. Nothing came close to her old one, so she bought a handful of replacements and tried to forget all about her special pen. Time passed and sure enough she started to think less about her precious pen. She managed to patch things up with her flatmates who forgave her for lashing out and giving them the silent treatment. She wished she could have handled things better, and resolved to do things differently in future.

A few months later she bashed a hoover into the sofa trying to manoeuvre it behind a chair leg. Something rolled out onto the carpet. She gasped and started dancing around the living room furniture, unable to contain herself! Staring back was none other than her lost pen. She was so delighted she picked it up and cradled it in her hands for a few minutes before resolving to put it away somewhere safe. Somewhere she could look after it more carefully…"

A phone rang and interrupted the author talk. I excused myself from the room and headed back to the unmanned reception desk. Just as I answered, Nicola entered the building and came bungling up the steps towards me. She started shouting "Go on Jason!" It was Barbara from Local on the other end, asking who was doing breaks.

"I'm not sure Barbara; look I'm so sorry but I'll have to go, something's just come up. You could try looking on the rota in the staff room."

"Hi Nicola, how are you today?"

"I'm doing Jason! Jason; I'm doing Jason!...number 5 please?"

"I'm sorry Nicola but none of the machines are available until tomorrow morning. There's an event in the computer room, an author talk. It's far busier than we thought it would be so the whole room is out of action. I can book you on number 5 for Wednesday morning though?"

Nicola was like Jed Maxwell, Alan Partridge's number one fan. Jed had a shrine plastered with all kinds of memorabilia and a giant tattoo of Alan's face that he'd spent fourteen hours on. Unlike Jed, Nicola's obsession was with Jason Donovan, circa 1989.

I'll send you all my dreams, every day in a letter...

"OK, so that's number 5 booked for Wednesday morning at eleven."

A LAST BEAUTY

A little over 10 years ago I bought a ticket to the Lake District with the last of my funds. No-one would ever find me. I paid the fare in cash and left no trail. I switched off the phone and gave away my last bags of stuff to charity shops. The escape was almost complete. My last adventure. By the time I arrived at Windermere it was late afternoon and the swollen grey clouds were predictably full of rain. I idled out of the station, past all the cabs perched in a row. There was an open top bus waiting outside the supermarket, complete with hordes of fresh faced tourists heading straight for the top deck. Suckers! I thought to myself. They'll need webbed feet and sturdy umbrellas to survive up here.

Crossing over the busy junction of the A591 and A5074 at the top of the High Street, I found the white 'Footpath to Orrest Head' sign on a dry stone wall. A twenty minute walk to the top promised unrivalled views of the Lake District Fells, Lake Windermere, Morecambe Bay and the Pennines. The first sight of mountains for many, the Lakes weren't the beginning of something; for me they were supposed to be the complete opposite…

I had the viewpoint to myself. Looking west to northwest from the summit I could just about make out the uprooted middle of Crinkle Crags, Scafell Pike, Bowfell, Great End, Great Gable and the Langdale Pikes. The glittering lights of Windermere and Bowness shimmered like glowing coals below and I started to think back to my first moment here, aged 13. Three of us on an ill-thought out bike ride from Lytham St. Annes to Bowness and back. A gruelling 132 mile trip in one day! I remembered calling my brother from one of Scott's iconic red phone boxes in Bowness, pleading with him to come and pick us up. He didn't. I think it was about 11.30pm when we eventually made it back. A trio of famished cavaliers, slowed to a crawl under total darkness with soulless bodies and throbbing bones.

Feeling a little disorientated, I rubbed my eyes and backtracked to a dry stone wall that followed a track into woodland. Through a blur of trees, I thought I could see a couple start to emerge. Bundled up in matching puffers, the man was on trend in a blue North Face jacket, while the woman nailed winter chic in red. They greeted me with a cheery 'Hello' as I stumbled past them. Heading north for a little while longer, I reached an opening above a small group of farm buildings. Tripping awkwardly over a stile, I ignored the 'Private Keep Out' sign and flopped down on an outcrop of sedimentary rock surrounded by sheep. Mudstones, sandstones, siltstones and limestone formed in the sea millions of years ago. Undisturbed by even the most distant sound of traffic, I stroked the folds and faults, pushed up and eroded from darkness until dawn, while casting trembling glances over the 10 mile expanse of Windermere. My headache was getting pretty severe, but the sky had cleared to a spectacular reddish colour. A last beauty awakened, my breathing slowed and I drifted off to sleep as though falling to the bottom of a lake. Through decaying plant and animal matter, I looked up to see rippling waves reflecting light back at me. At that moment, I could not have denied the exaltations of an under-presence. While I drifted along the lake bed an ever-growing swishing sound rose like fireworks, until a crown of gold flashed overhead. Spotlights shone into the water while my soul floated with the music. I moved forward, opened my arms, and fell into my own reflection, disappearing beneath the surface of the water.

CHAINED TO THE POT WASH

They kept me in for a few days afterwards. I didn't want the folks or anyone else to know, so I was referred to a 'crisis' house. Even though I wasn't supposed to stay overnight, they let me sleep there on and off for months on end. They usually gave me a little en-suite room that I barricaded myself into. The staff were kind and gave out gifts too, mostly generic items, bookmarks with inspirational messages and contact details of support organisations. Amongst all the chaos and confusion, I managed to get some much needed cash together after pleading poverty to my ex-flatmate. Most days I gravitated toward the library, a magnet offering snippets of human contact and support. In modern times I guess I would have been hooked up with a counsellor and given a safety plan with an app I agreed to follow. Back then a culture of ambivalence was still prevalent and complicated matters considerably. After a while, like an addict drifting along the junk road, I learnt there was no key or secret that anyone could give you. You couldn't just wake up one morning and decide that everything was ok. It could take years and even then you still didn't know if or when the 'dead moods' would return. To start again with a slate wiped clean. I guess it was inevitable I had to try again at some point. Holed up in the Lakes, this meant undertaking a variety of hospitality jobs. At first I found them severely draining and seriously underpaid. I wasn't much use as a barista, so I ended up chained to the pot wash on 4-6 hour shifts throughout the busiest part of the day. I just about managed to cope with the relentless volley of dirty dishes, cooking utensils, glasses and coffee cups. Mostly piled high on a miniscule sink area by a team of stressed out multi-national gofers. You had to get them clean quickly so that all the pots and pans were available as soon as possible. Hot and manic, I didn't have much time to stop my thoughts running out of control.

There were always jobs going in the summer months and they were all the same. Part-time, fixed term or seasonal, an endless merry-go-round of exploitative establishments offering labour-intensive and pressurised roles. Long hours with no job security. Eventually, I exchanged the pot wash for a string of front of house positions in galleries and cafés with large side orders of family melodrama. My initiation included working three jobs at once for the National Trust. In particular, a fraught six month stretch stuck on the front door of Beatrix Potter's house. Both property managers had disappeared early into my spell after it was alleged they'd made inappropriate remarks about Japanese visitors. This left me exposed to an army of retired volunteers, a comic bunch like a Who's Who of Dick Emery's TV creations. Barry and Roy, a pair of effeminate swingers patrolled the upstairs landing area and who referred to everyone as either 'Ducky' or 'Darling'. Cathy, a frustrated spinster (like the character 'Hettie' one of Emery's best-known comic creations) wore a suit inspired by Beatrix's wedding dress, made entirely out of Herdwick wool.

Working on the edges of tourism, I found it hard to develop any long lasting connections to either the people or the land itself. I lived in the attic room of a large shared house in the centre of one of the main towns. The accommodation had been divvied up into several rooms and contained a pick and mix of locals and folk from Eastern Europe. Most of the time, everyone stayed in their room, even those with families in tow. Occasionally, I snuck out of my ivory tower and crept downstairs to the communal kitchen area to check if any of the washing machines were free. While the seasons passed, I communed with song birds as they perched on chimneys and aerials up and down the road. Night after night, reflective and peaceful, the liquid gold refrains echoed throughout neighbouring woods before sinking behind distant hills. I got the job at the library after offering to volunteer at one of the smaller branches. I'd overheard a tourist complaining about opening hours to a member of staff. They tried to explain how short staffed they were, which often led to the sudden closure of branches. Unfortunately, this occurred without much notice, which was the nature of the complaint. At first I helped out once a week with shelving and tidying before I carved out a niche as the resident IT wiz. Eventually, I was offered a zero hours position after a council restructure stripped out all the senior library assistants and children's librarians.

MASKED DISCONTENT

There was extensive coverage of the 70th anniversary of the liberation of Auschwitz on the news channels. To mark the occasion, a giant white tent had been set up over the Gate of Death at the Birkenau II camp. Nearly 300 survivors from Poland and across the world attended the commemoration, many making their way through the snow to lay candles at the Memorial. Also present were more than 50 leaders of countries and international organisations who gathered solemnly to hear from some of the witnesses.

Some ten months later, the Paris shootings added an extra layer to the world's collective trauma. Hardly a day seemed to pass without reports of more barbaric forms of brutality. Everyday existence revolved around symbolic and sacrificial bombings, beheadings or shootings. Rooted in this culture of death was a long phony war of *no contest*.

It made me think back to 'the mother of all events' that day in the General Manager's office. And that silence when the images were being played over and over on the TV screens. I can still hear Maestro's words while everybody looked on in astonishment, alarmed by the outside world.

"We've been shaken out of our collective slumber man. Everyone needs to question what he or she is doing, in order to see just how bad things are. This is the 'masked discontent' Fanon spoke of, the smoking ashes of a burnt-down house, which threaten to burst into flames again."

BREAKING POINT

"I think Boris has been something of a damp squib so far. We need some of Nigel's thunderflashes to stir things up!"

Sometimes four of them sat around the square white table next to Dave's office. Always complaining, they leaned back in their chairs and flicked through magazines and papers while cheering on their villainous spiv. With the referendum fast approaching, anything to do with immigration, welfare, agriculture and fishing was fair game, all within earshot of the reception desk.

"I'm sick of all the Cameronites scaremongering, makes me more determined than ever to vote out!"

To most people, Peter introduced himself as both an undiscovered artist and an art historian. As if to emphasise the point, a 1995 Phaidon hardback edition of Ernst Gombrich's *The Story of Art* accompanied him everywhere.

"The art world is always looking for fully formed artists, mature artists, serious artists. I'm not going to burn out as sometimes happens with these young'uns… and my prices are cheap, dirt cheap in fact. So I'm offering value for money."

In his early sixties, he always wore the same light grey mac, with a dark green sweatshirt underneath, charcoal coloured chinos and a pair of old brown loafers, that should have been certified dead years ago. Dried up and skinny, with a grey face hidden behind a pair of horn-rimmed specs, he sported a grizzled saucepan haircut. Apparently he'd been laid off from his old bookkeeping job at a family run gallery in less than favourable circumstances. Since then he'd been coming in every day, job hunting, looking at art books while trying to ruffle a few feathers.

"I pray we Brexit. If we don't then I will lose the will."

Dave was the caretaker/handyman for our group of libraries. Even though he was only meant to use the little office next to the workroom as a base, he hardly ever left it and certainly never went to any other branches. Born and bred in London, he was the ultimate ex-forces media cliché; covered in tattoos with a shaved head and a low, breathy rasp similar to his namesake, the long-suffering barman of the Winchester Club from the TV series *Minder*. Pride had taken a hit recently when his much-prized BMW 3-series stencilled with a flag of St George had been stolen from under his nose!

"And I'll tell you something - the bastards had the cheek to arrive at my place in a stolen Corsa! Still can't believe I was awoken by the sound of my own motor… and then to watch it being driven down the road. That's taking the piss. The coppers said they drove in a convoy all the way down the M6 towards Birmingham!"

Peter cut in…

"Ere – have you seen this new poster 'Breaking Point?' Could be the queue to vote out on the 23rd!"

After dealing with a bus pass enquiry, I noticed Peter and Dave had been joined by big Geoff, another specialist in hollow rhetoric.

"Not long til polling day Geoff!"

Geoff pulled out a chair with his filthy hands. He always looked big and dirty with a ratty face, baggy out-of-date clothes and a mild, muffled voice.

"I've just seen that poster on the news. I wish all the left wing do-gooders would take their heads out of the sand and get a grip! If you remove 100,000 'refugees' from our houses then you'd have 100,000 houses for the indigenous, it's simple common sense!"

"I agree big man and these are the ones that steal our jobs….whilst also stealing our benefits…come to think of it, that's talent!"

I noticed a surprisingly wistful look begin to form on Peter's face as he gazed out of the open windows and sat watching a set of drifting clouds set sail upon a little camp of blue.

THERE ARE ONLY ARTISTS

Next day back at the library, I bumped into Peter who was standing beside the photocopier. He noticed I was carrying an old Eugène Delacroix journal while juggling a pile of other artist books.

"Looks a handful, something important?"

"It's another staple of art history education Peter - all 700 odd pages of it. In addition to being an excellent artist, Delacroix's writing is supposedly a joy to read. Someone's requested his journal; I've just been down to the reserve stack to retrieve it."

"Didn't he do *The Raft of the Medusa* or was that someone else? I can never remember their names correctly."

"That was a different French painter, called Géricault. I actually remember seeing the painting in the Red Rooms of the Louvre years and years ago. It's very impressive and massive too."

But Peter didn't seem too impressed holding onto his copying and squinting at the cover of the journal.

"I'll have to look it up in my big book, bound to be in there somewhere. Do you know what the very first line of it is? There really is no such thing as Art...There are only artists - I like the emphasis on image making. Still, makes me wonder why an artist feels compelled to make art, or whatever you want to call it. Is it because they have to. Or is it so that it's seen, admired and praised?"

"They probably come hand-in-hand Peter don't you think?"

"What I really mean is, I just don't get all this pretentious modern rubbish. I've seen it in the papers when they talk about that annual freak show down in London. Grey circles painted on black backgrounds, pieces of tarp hung by scotch tape or a screwed up ball of printer paper. Come on, where is the skill in that? And people pay ludicrous sums for it. It doesn't bear comparison with say, the Pre-Raphaelites."

Using the copier as a stand-in counter, I decided to indulge him by combing through a selection of colour plates from the other books I had on me.

"There are plenty of folk who think if I could have done it - then it's not art. What about artists such as Mark Rothko or Jack the Dripper, the so-called Abstract Expressionists? Surely you must appreciate big colour field works along with Pollock's free-flowing jazzy numbers?"

Peter lifted up his glasses and looked breathless as his speech rippled with anger...

"It would appear if you can throw a bucket of paint over a large enough canvas and commit suicide afterwards then you'll become immortal and make an absolute packet for your grandkids."

BACK INTO THE PIT

We all have the power of life or death. It's a choice that confronts each of us every day. To be honest, I'd managed to block it out until it had begun to sneak its way back in with the return of the falling dreams. Then I couldn't avoid considering the consequences for all living things, no matter how big or small. Even if it meant an intervention, like the time I tripped over trying to avoid squashing a whirligig beetle on the riverside path. Wandering the circular route during my lunch breaks, the graceful swans weaved silently along the banks. Floating through a carpet of petals, in and out of the willow trees whose branches respectfully bowed to stroke the water. With views of ancient bridges, I sometimes stopped at the Grade 1 listed church to take it all in. Nearby, a line of ancient trees would soon be marked for death. On this occasion, the circling shiny black oval shaped insect with orange legs survived.

On the whole, I tried to avoid killing things. Nowadays, I'd even consider myself an honourable person. I have a short tumbler with a piece of card on standby to untangle bees from the sticky goo of greedy spiders. I won't deny such attempts to nurture anything toward the special apparatus will often try my patience to its very limit. And whenever anything is successfully released back into the world I shudder at the thought of it rushing recklessly back into the pit.

SEALED WITH A KISS

Every morning at the stroke of 11am Nicola would be standing at the reception desk. She always wanted to be on the same computer, so it was of vital importance to make sure number 5 was booked out to her. Otherwise the consequences could be catastrophic. On Mondays, Wednesdays and Fridays she came straight from a Community Development Association drop-in at the shopping centre over the road. Sometimes she brought a younger chap called Stuart who attended the same sessions. He always carried a string of rosary beads and was much taller than her; he must have been well over 6ft. His main passion involved watching episodes of Postman Pat! The children's favourite postie with a cute black and white cat called Jess.

"Pat! Jess! Jason! Go on Jason!"

Sometimes the pair of them sat side-by-side yelling out nonsense above the regular buzz of people answering phones, getting into arguments and swearing at other patrons.

No one seemed to know how or why Nicola's obsession had developed. It only centred on one of his songs, a cover version of The Four Voices song *Sealed with a Kiss*. Over her allotted two hour stints, she played the YouTube video on repeat, sometimes singing along with a voice that sounded like a train pulling into a station. Written in 1960 by Gary Geld and Peter Udell, the track was considered to be the archetypal American highschool teen love song. Two lovers go their separate ways at the end of summer, while the narrator promises to send his love and dreams in daily letters. In the video, her hero sits beside a camp fire, mournful and coiffured in the waning afterglow of Stock Aitken and Waterman's slew of avaricious pop heat.

Nicola had wavy shoulder length dark hair, centre parted with blonde highlights. Aged forty, she was cigarette shaped with the face of an absent child. She usually wore a royal blue duffle jacket with light grey jogging bottoms and a pair of unloved, worn and useless plimsolls. She could turn on the water works whenever she wanted anything. Particularly if we encountered any problems printing the endless images of Jason cut and pasted from her favourite video.

Generally speaking, she was reasonably well behaved as long as she put on her headphones and escaped into the world of obsessive fandom. On rare occasions, she abandoned Jason to gaze dolefully at East Coast Main Line timetables from London to Edinburgh. A cog in the wheel of the UK's ultimate travel experience. She told me on several occasions that her old man used to be a train driver. Apparently, he lived near to Kings Cross on the infamous Brutalist Weston Rise housing estate. Once renowned as a 'haven for drug barons, junkies and prostitutes', it opened with much fanfare in 1961 and contained similar characteristics to the Park Hill Estate, Sheffield. Nicola always reminded me that I shared the same name as her old man. He's dead now though. I'm not sure how he died and to be honest, I didn't dare ask.

The other thing I noticed her watching occasionally was news footage connected with the murder of Lee Rigby. The Fusilier who was run down and butchered by two men as he walked back to his barracks on the streets of Woolwich, South East London in 2013. A public act of 'just do it terrorism' designed to inspire Jihadist drifters the world over. I'm not quite sure what the fascination was, but Bev (one of the other part-timers who vaguely knew Nicola's Mum), reckoned the area must have had connections to her Dad.

DANGER ZONE

We only had about 10 or 15 minutes to get everything ready for opening the library. Everyone would go through their own routines, switching on lights, the public PCs, self-issue machines, opening blinds, taking the cash drawer out of the safe, logging on to the catalogue and checking emails etc. Part of my morning procedure always involved laying out an ever decreasing number of newspapers on the reading room table. On one occasion I was drawn to a headline about the former residents in the ghost city of Pripyat. Some 30 years on from the nuclear disaster at Chernoybl, the abandoned Ukrainian metropolis had been declared unsafe for 24,000 years.

'Heroes of the Soviet Union' - the honour bestowed upon evacuees and workers who returned to the devastating inferno to fight the fires. In 1986, the future was so bright you had to wear shades along with a blue worker's boiler suit and slippers. This was the same year that saw the Soviet's launch the Mir Space Station, the disaster of the Space Shuttle Challenger and in dear ol' Blighty Fergie got hitched to Prince Andrew. On the Top Gun soundtrack, Kenny Loggins took us high into the "Danger Zone."

After opening the main doors, I went straight over to unload the trolley next to the self-issue. It was then I noticed someone had just returned a copy of Coupland's *Generation X*.

"Been a long time…" I said without thinking as I picked it up and quickly skimmed through my former companion until the pages fell open at the start of the 'Monsters Exist' chapter.

'Radioactive!' I started to read the bit where Dag drops the jar of Trinitite from Alamogordo, 'where they had the first N-test…'

"Excuse me, do you work here?"

I looked up at a bronzed skin lady, her yellowy hair glittering in the sunlight.

"Yes, how can I help?"

"Where do I return this?"

She was holding a hardback of Harper Lee's second novel *Go Set a Watchman*.

"Not a problem, I can do that for you on the self-issue."

Within moments, I was back to Dag's episode with the bottle of plutonium in Claire's house. When the green glass beads explode and shoot *everywhere*. I picked up my old friend and sought refuge on one of the pods a little out of the glare of the opening rush.

'Possibly the most charmed object in my collection…'

Almost the same words Johnny used to describe his own bottle of radioactive dust. Before I moved to South East London, I rented a dishevelled flat with him and a South African couple on the fringes of the green belt. It was in a quaint little village above a set of shops directly opposite the Green Man. The pub was hardly a symbol of rebirth though. Trapped in our own minds the habits took hold while any other interests lost all importance. A modern melancholy poetic where eyes began to close and everything started to go through the motions. Johnny and I were embroiled in the infinite merry-go-round of writing, rehearsing, and recording and gigging having played in bands for years. His uncle was 'the poodle' bass player/lead singer from 80's new wave synth pop combo Kajagoogoo. With spiky hair and androgynous looks, their name came to be synonymous with a multitude of other one-hit wonders. Johnny played bass like his uncle, but nourished himself more on the kick of drugs and booze than filling the cap with infectious grooves. He thought of himself as a real ladies man being half-Greek with dark curly hair, a slim build and large brown eyes, perfect for his much rehearsed 'little boy lost' look. "Can I cane?" There was usually someone to sponge money and fags off before he moved onto the next unsuspecting victim.

Johnny was infatuated by the fictional character Tony Montana from Brian De Palma's 1983 film, *Scarface*. Part of the 125,000 Marielitos as the Cuban refugees came to be known, who landed in Florida with nothing. A mass exodus driven by the Cold War politics of a stagnant economy weakened under the grip of the U.S. trade embargo and Castro's irritation with detractors. After retiring himself as a dishwasher, Tony climbs the ranks of the criminal underworld to become one of the most powerful drug lords in Miami. It was probably the twisted rags to riches version of the American Dream that appealed most to Johnny. His fascination with the magnetism of the criminal world would become his undoing. He enjoyed referring to his old man as Shotgun Lou after an unsavoury incident with a rowdy bunch of hooligans. The episode took place at the chip shop owned by his father near Wimbledon FC's old ground on Plough Lane. Johnny helped him out a couple of nights a week and usually headed onto a few clubs afterwards. It was during this period that he started to frequent the Blue Orchid night club in South East London. Formerly known as the Croydon Greyhound, that once hosted bands like The Damned and The Buzzcocks. The two-discotheque club was owned by Charlie Kray who ran it until 1997 just before he was jailed for a second time. A Met Police sting operation uncovered his involvement in smuggling millions of pounds worth of cocaine into Surrey and London. Johnny referred to him as 'his friend Charlie' and always maintained that he was charming and friendly. No one knew how he had got to know him, but Johnny always proudly displayed, *Villains We Have Known* a book penned by Charlie's infamous younger brother Reg. A product of the environment with his identical twin brother Ron (alias The Colonel), The Twins ruled the East End with their gang The Firm throughout the 1950s and 1960s. The paperback was signed by Charlie, and included a message dedicated to Johnny, 'The World is Yours…'

'Radioactive!' Johnny claimed to have received a jar of dust particles from Chernobyl off one of Charlie's hard-nosed geezers at the Blue Orchid. It festered somewhere in-amongst all the other piles of junk scattered around his bedroom. On the door he'd blu-tacked a crude mock-up of the '25 Cromwell Street' sign.

One Monday evening in winter time about 6pm, I arrived back to an empty flat. I'd been away for the weekend at the folks' place near Brighton. After opening the door, I quickly realised the entire place was shrouded in darkness. No one had fed the meter. Thankfully, a small play of light shone through the hallway and guided me to the kitchen at the far end. While I was feeling inside the drawers trying to locate a candle and some matches, a series of loud bangs on the front door interrupted my rummaging. It turned out to be a drugs raid, with four police officers responding to a tip-off from an unknown source at the Green Man. Even though it was murky, I could tell the two men were dressed in plain clothes while the women officers wore the traditional crisp uniform with high-vis vests. They thought I was bluffing about the electricity situation at first, but after testing a few switches one of them went racing downstairs and soon returned with a couple of torches. They turned my room inside out and found nothing. While they were having a quick debrief, I stood in the shadowy hallway, staring up at Johnny's door. It made me nervous to think what kind of substances might be lurking in there. They split into pairs and began searching the remaining two bedrooms.

"I've got something here!"

One of them called out in a whiny, voice. He emerged like a spaceman from the gloom of Johnny's bear pit shaking a jar filled with something dark brown.

All five of us gathered in the hallway as he offered

the find up to the search lights.

"What is it?"

"Looks quite smooth"

"Taste it"

"Careful, could be a bad bundle"

He shook the jar again and showed it to me.

"Come on, you must know what it is."

Like a faraway memory slowly surfacing, I could hear Johnny's laughter lunging through the air, beating tentative wings along the walls.

"If I told you the truth, you would never believe me."

Months later, Johnny was arrested for trying to pass counterfeit twenties at the local Esso garage. We'd all long moved out by the time he was sentenced. I heard he got something like 120 hours community service. Typically, instead of doing his penance he ended up disappearing to charm magic America. Chasing his dream in the land of opportunity with the tradition of finding any way possible to get what you want in life. Johnny the Greek we nicknamed him. No doubt I will never see him again…

PART THREE

| May 2016 |

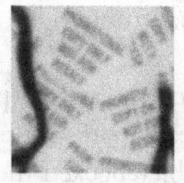

ZERO HOURS

There's been a turn for the worse.
You MUST get here as soon as possible.
Please do try xx

I awoke in the near dark. The first thing I saw were lights going on and off. The pattern repeated ad infinitum. I moved my eyes from side to side, but everything seemed different. It was as if nothing was real anymore. Take the grey Herdy mug on the bedside table, something about it just didn't look right. None of the other objects in the bedroom did either. Even though they were all in exactly the same place, I couldn't quite put my finger on what made them seem so different. I tried hard to think about it, nothing sprung to mind, and so I closed my eyes again. Back into the repetitive cycle of contradictions, a simple truth that wraps happiness and anxiety into a single gesture. The day's divinity and voices were all around me. I came to again and heard the reassuring three familiar pings. The old spice whistle brought a realisation that it must have been a dream. Gently, I leant across and held the screen up to my face. After staring at the wall at the foot of the bed for a moment, I got up, threw some clothes on and went to brush my teeth. The familiar wrinkles in the mirror didn't bring their usual regrets today. I smiled to myself… so things were the same, I was still visibly ageing. Turning to leave,

I noticed how the bathroom light shimmered faintly in the mirror.

At the foot of the stairs I paused to change the timer and turn the heating off. Despite the settings it hadn't come on. I double-checked the control to no avail. In the kitchen, I opened the fridge door and thrust my head in then made a coffee and buttered some toast, before speeding off in the car. If the motorway traffic behaved properly for once, I could be there around mid to late afternoon. The thing was, I'd no idea what I'd be met with on arrival. Part of me hoped I'd be too late. I turned right at the Swan Hotel, onto the A591 and the exit from Grasmere village was soon behind me. At the tight left-hand corner at Penny Rock Wood by Loughrigg Fell, I was distracted by an atmospheric glow through the trees. Thank God there was nothing coming on the other side of the road otherwise I could have hit them head on. Rubbing my eyes in an effort to banish this sudden radiance, I skirted by a tranquil Rydal without mishap. Through a cool jewelled Ambleside on the way to a series of snaking bends that led to the Low Wood. There didn't seem much on the road for a June morning.

Before hitting the M6, I pulled over into an empty lay-by. I needed to send a quick text to my boss asking her to arrange cover. I knew Friday was her day off, but thought she'd understand the urgency of my request once she knew the reason. You never knew what the reaction would be to any impromptu holiday requests. Normally, timing was everything. Any such attempts required raising the subject at precisely the right moment. Besides, I was on a zero hour contract and most of the time she hadn't a clue when I was supposed to be in. Shaken by the wind, the sky drew close like curtains round a bed.

WATFORD GAP

I got on to the M6 just before ten o'clock. It took me a while before I realised practically all the other lanes were empty. Normally they'd have been bursting with nameless hordes. At least that meant I could make some real progress until the dreary thud of Stafford's new Smart motorway upgrade. After nearly an hour the speed limit dropped abruptly from sixty to twenty as the road works duly arrived. A little drowsy as the car slowed to a crawl, the push button windows provided me with a temporary distraction. I pressed them randomly, and only a minute or two later decided to scan for new radio stations instead. The lead for the iPod got tangled round the gear stick after I'd chucked it onto the passenger seat. Ignoring this trivial hindrance, I felt inside the door trim panel with frantic fingers searching for any cassettes that hadn't been played in a while.

Occasionally I glanced at my phone screen. No new messages. I even leant back and closed my eyes at one point, grunting myself awake with a series of eye watering yawns. Enveloped in solitude, I blew my nose, rubbed my eyes and adjusted the seat cushion. When the road works came to an end, I put my foot down as I moved further south. Even the weather started to pick up after the woolpack of clouds that had wrapped and cradled my car from Cumbria dissolved into cerulean skies. In the dead calm, a new kind of transparent blue seemed to intensify the glare from the bonnet. When I eventually pulled in at Watford Gap it was nearing three o'clock in the afternoon.

HOT OR COLD WITH THAT?

As I suspected, there were hardly any other vehicles when I pulled up opposite the entrance. The only noise reverberating throughout the glass atrium came from a Postman Pat ride merrily rocking up and down. Everyone's favourite in the unseen network of friends, enemies and romancers. I headed off to the Gents, scooting past a number of empty cubicles until I settled on one at the far end. Burying my nose as usual in a t-shirt sleeve to try and block out the strong smell of sewage. Afterwards, I wandered into a fully stocked WH Smiths and left the money for a paper beside the till. Further along I stopped to study the vast array of delicacies on offer at Costa. With open hands raised high above my head, I looked in awe at all the sweet and savoury pastries, wraps and summer fancies. I'd choose a White Americano without a second thought normally faced with such infinite possibilities. Coughing tentatively into my curled right hand, I looked up and was startled to see a young girl smiling back across the counter. She was tall and dark with a thin foreign looking face.

"Hello sir. How are you doing today? What can I get for you? By the way, did you know we've been voted the nation's favourite coffee shop for the third year in a row? Will you be drinking the perfect cup inside or on the go today sir? Oh and whilst you're there, would you like to fill in our new one minute survey for the chance to win a gift card worth £100?"

The combination of her effusive charm and the

textures swirling round in the milk jug only made my head spin. All of a sudden, she banged the jug down on the counter with a thud and clipped -

"Hot or cold with that sir?"

My cheeks grew warm, so I picked up a serviette and padded them.

"er…yes, I don't mind."

Breathing loudly, I decided to head off immediately and sip the coffee en route. A slight drizzle was falling as I pulled out toward the blue exit sign on the slip road. The atmosphere had turned overcast again and I thought of rainstorms and the dripping ceiling in the dark cave I rented. For the first time in ages, I'd forgotten to put buckets out in the rush to get away. I knew that whenever I returned, the special acidic reek, a festering pulp that moved in your throat and caused nostrils to dilate would be waiting.

"Poo-tee-weet?" I said slowly, staring up at the grey sky where the birds were talking to each other.

THE MUD-CHOKED WASTELAND

Thankfully the M25 flowed reasonably well around Heathrow with few tailbacks for once. When I eventually arrived in Brighton the shadows on the pavements outside the Royal Pavilion had started to lengthen. I wondered whether I'd still be in time after noticing it had crept beyond 5pm as I passed the clock tower at the end of Palace Pier. Turning left at Bedford Street, then right onto Eastern Road, finding a space in the endless labyrinth of the subterranean County Hospital car park took another 15 minutes. After clambering out of the driver's seat, I stood still for a minute or two, holding my lower back until a sharp pinch in my left shoulder blade disappeared. Shifting from left foot to right foot, a sudden queasiness formed in the pit of my stomach.

The car park had been built on top of a steep incline. This I only realised when exiting the lift. Directly opposite, the path skewed sharply downwards toward the main hospital buildings. I had to tilt my head back to appreciate a wrecking ball attached to a crane adorned with the blue NHS logo. It had been plonked down in front of a muddy vintage dominating the sky like a Brutalist high-rise. Brown and bare and abandoned in the open gap it stood there seeping blood like a dead weight in a sling...

"The diggers and the tower cranes."

A single point of entry to the building led to a man-made crater that was seemingly fashioned from a network of trenches. Like a flower opened wide, the scars of the Great War entombed on an island of unclaimed bodies. In nervous systems and bones, the human body is itself another battleground, where bacteria, viruses and parasites wait to multiply. I bent down and slowly tied my shoelaces. While studying the mud-choked wasteland I'd completely lost my bearings. I stood up and held my hands close to my chest. A group of four or five medical staff in regulation white coats caught me by surprise. Their purposeful gait and cohesion proved a magnet I couldn't resist. Beware the men in white coats! The time had come again. Even though they were moving at a brisk pace, I managed to tag along behind as they skirted the crater. I soon lost them after they turned right at a large stop sign. Following on regardless, I turned into a white stone building with a dark grey sliding entrance that was cross-shaped. Behind this another set of doors was bathed in burnt orange. These swung open into a narrow corridor, and I strode in, hesitating at a snazzy new sign with the words, Frontier Pathology. Written in slate-hued capitals, I noticed how the *nt* in the word Frontier was bolder than the other letters.

The loud footsteps of a male nurse carrying a clipboard and set of sterile containers approached rapidly behind. Without saying a word he stopped and motioned back to where I'd come in, before he sped off down another corridor. Ignoring a glass sliding door temptingly positioned to the right, I followed in his direction before picking up the signs for reception. There I stopped at the desk and waited for the receptionist to finish blathering on about fire regulations down the phone.

"Doctor - Why didn't you answer me when I called? Hmm...I've no idea who is responsible for fire safety legislation."

SIMPLY BOTIFUL

Lit by a small pair of fluorescent tubes, the clock had stopped above a desk the shape of a piece of Trivial Pursuit cheese. Feeling the burn from the tubes overhead I stared at the lovely, rich sheen of the counter's creamy white timber. It reminded me of the unbound maple neck of my first guitar. With a Rosewood "skunk" stripe, the body neck recess was stamped "TL-69 PRD." While everyone (including myself) thought of it as a Pink Paisley Tele, Fender always called it Paisley Red (or "PRD"). It was love at first sight after I'd seen the guitarist from Doctor and the Medics with one on Top of the Pops. I still couldn't believe how I'd managed to cobble enough cash together to join in with all the pseudo-psychedelia. Suddenly a sharp buzzing noise came from a pair of double doors behind me. Glancing upwards, I noticed a staircase with a picture of a refrigerator door painted in mint green. I looked hard at it for a moment and then back at the receptionist. Closing an eye, I saw Christoph Blücher's mysterious installation *Simply Botiful* at Hauser & Wirth's Coppermill gallery off Brick Lane. Decked out as a low-rent fleabox, a sleazy mise-en-scene consisted of threadbare, carpeted stairs that led up into a passageway with offices and bedrooms. Thunderous metal riffs blasted from a stereo in a corridor lined with makeshift bunks. One room was stuffed with fossils and exotic animal bones like an anthropologist or archaeologist's study, while the end of the passage overlooked a huge warehouse. An electrical knacker's yard contained several metal portacabins, around which were stacks of disused refrigerators, broken TVs, VCRs and radios. Down the stairs, narrow pathways twisted between dizzying columns of fridges, wiring strata and circuit board landslides. An immersive large scale film set with faint hints of narrative, such as the smell of empty beer bottles or an assortment of pages torn from porno mags and then stuck to the walls of the portacabins. On from the vast warehouse, the setting changed to piles of CDs, boxes of vinyl and disused computer equipment in a mouldy smelling office. An old refrain swept through - 'Anywhere will do, just keep the junk out of the boardroom...'

There was an offsite storage area plastered head to toe in porn images the same as Blucher's piece. In another coincidence, I installed a fridge in the stockroom opposite the record company offices during my first week, only to leave it behind a few years later. For all I knew, my former cold companion could be hiding out somewhere amongst the secret histories of Blücher's imitation Bangla Town.

I scanned my phone agitatedly for a further minute or two while I waited for the receptionist to hang up.

"You were talking away there," I looked over the desk when she finally finished.

"Sorry," she said and straightened up on her chair.

Scrolling through the patient database, she mumbled a few details back at me.

I didn't say anything and leant forward trying to focus on her voice. While jiggling the car ignition key in my jacket pocket, I couldn't help but notice how quickly she manoeuvred the mouse around on a tiny pad curled on two sides. She stopped for a second and took off a big pair of brown glasses…

"Yes, it's Chichester Ward. No new developments."

I stared at her specs before the glowing tubes burnt into my eyes.

She stood up and moved away from the desk pointing back down the corridor.

"Go through the double doors on your left and take the lift on the right to the third floor. Turn left when you come out, head round the corner and up the slope. You'll see the entrance to the ward ahead. You can't miss it."

"Thank you," I said at last, trying to gather a smile at the same time.

"You're welcome," she said, laying a hand on the top of the desk.

OL' BLUE EYES

I rang the door buzzer and waited for the ward clerk to finish opening the drapes of a venetian blind. He was having difficulty raising it without a clatter. The clerk's desk appeared to be hemmed in by four patients ashen with the sickly pallor of corpses. The clerk took my shoulder in silence and guided me past a few beds around a corner to the right. He said something but I wasn't listening. I'd already caught sight of my sister standing by a chair next to a curtained-off bed. She looked heavier with her hair whiter than I remembered and as wavy as the waves I'd driven past on the seafront. The ward had that sick room mustiness, replete with the smell of medicines, antiseptic and artificial fragrances. Shutting the windows meant all these contradictions fused together. My sister was sniffling and sad as she took my hand and motioned me to sit down.

"It's not good. You'd better prepare yourself."

I squeezed her fingers gently, "Don't worry, I'll be fine."

Rising from the chair I pulled the curtain back and nodded to my brother sitting by the top of the bed. He looked serious in a dark grey suit, but his cheeks were as pale as the bed sheets and he kept rolling his tongue repeatedly over his teeth. The body lying down had a contorted face and was almost completely drained of colour save for a mild yellow tinge to the forehead. A set of drips had been inserted into a right arm imprinted with a rainbow of colours; mottled like the luminous surface of a plum. A number of pillows were puffed and raised so that the body arched forward. Every so often a groan solidified into a wall. My brother tried to reassure the noise…

"It's alright, it's alright. We're all here now."

I couldn't think of anything to add. So I just stood there in stony silence. Gulping, my sister poked her head round the curtain.

"You ok?"

"Yes. Why wouldn't I be?" I couldn't help snapping at her. This I knew was daft as soon as I said it. Immediately I looked down at the floor and twitched nervously on my heels. A couple of minutes later, she came in and stood beside me.

"Would you like me to get another chair?"

I thought about it for a moment.

"No, I'm fine thanks. I'll be ok here for a minute."

Then my brother stood up and crawled along the side of the bed and out on to the ward. At that point my sister turned to me directly.

"How was the journey down? We were wondering what time you'd get here."

"Fine really, you wouldn't believe it, but there was hardly anything on the road," I replied dreamily.

She turned and looked at the bed.

"What are we going to do with you?" she whispered.

My brother returned and drew back the curtain. He had brought along a tall male nurse with hair black as coal. The nurse gestured for us to follow him into a small box room just off the ward.

"Please wait here whilst I go and fetch the consultant. She won't be a minute. She'd like to have a few words with you all."

His voice rose at the end and there was even the faintest trace of a lisp. He wandered off leaving us in the bare and stale smelling room. No windows, no pictures; only dark furniture silhouetted against patternless white wallpaper. By the door a water vending machine hummed briefly. Its screen displayed OUT OF ORDER in capitals, while a series of bubbles routinely discharged upwards.

It wasn't long before the consultant arrived. She was a young woman in her early thirties at most, slender with dark features and gentle green eyes. As the door closed she said,

"I hear someone's just travelled down from Cumbria?" She didn't speak for long and my sister sobbed as we left.

After that we gathered back at the bed. Mother arrived shortly afterwards just as the groaning sounds got louder and more frequent. In contrast to my sister, she appeared skeleton-like, her neck loose in the collar of her coat. Her skin was slightly jaundiced and lined, but even though her eyes were glazing over she hadn't lost her looks. My brother kept going off in search of doctors to supply more morphine. He always came back with the same answer.

"Apparently, there's no one available to issue any drugs!"

By now the clock had ticked round to regular visiting time. A nurse came and suggested moving into a more private room. But mother rapped at her,

"No, I don't want to be moved now. We'll stay

as we are thank you."

"And to think, he'd only been saying to me last night – I don't like it in here, when am I coming out?"

As she spoke I thought of how the prospect of being discharged would have only have brought a new set of challenges. Back at home, mother devoted all her time to caring for him. More often than not his erratic, childish behaviour overwhelmed her completely.

Unexpectedly the nurse came back with a portable CD player. She leant right across the bed to plug it in and put on some Frank Sinatra. She explained how background music had helped in a similar situation recently. I didn't know where mother had sloped off to, but when she reappeared the music stopped immediately. Ol' Blue Eyes didn't even make it to the first verse.

JUICY COUTURE

I stood up and moved away from the bed bumping straight into another nurse who'd come round with a trolley to check bins and take waste away. She was Asian, very petite and barely four and a half feet tall. I noticed 'Housekeeper' was printed on her staff badge in bold italics. She said she'd heard mother's raised voice and asked if everything was ok. Whispering softly to her, I spoke about the problems we faced,

"It's because she isn't really a carer. She finds it hard to come to terms with what is going on. There's a lot of frustration and pride."

The Housekeeper nodded before replying so quietly I could hardly hear her.

"It's the same with a lot of older people. Sometimes, they don't like asking for assistance; they just want to manage on their own."

She checked her watch and ran a hand through her hair. I moved a few steps further away from the bed, making sure she followed, and said,

"Thing is; I remember when we finally convinced mother to contact the council. All they did when they came round was install a few handrails in the bathroom and outside the front door. They also put in one of those panic alarm things – bloody thing was always going off in the middle of the night!"

The Housekeeper's cheeks flushed, but it was true. Mother only viewed help as a hindrance. She'd always tried to resist any offers of support. Plus, she resented the thought of having to pay for it. That's why things had got more and more difficult. The long distance between us didn't make it any easier.

Just after eight o'clock the consultant began her rounds with an oriental looking Doctor whose high cheekbones and smooth skin glinted off points of light in the ward. The groaning increased in volume and regularity. We knew it wouldn't be long. They administered another dose of morphine and spoke quietly with mother. Everyone looked drained, slumped into chairs with sweaty hands barely able to support weary heads. Sensing the fear my stomach churned over, whilst the pain in my lower back returned again. Desperate for air, I offered to go on a hunt for drinks. As I checked my wallet for change, my sister looked to the window.

"You may have to go outside if the shop's closed downstairs."

Leaving the ward I bounded down the spiral staircase that led to reception. Nearing the bottom steps I looked across the corridor to the closed metal shutter of the Spar. My sister hadn't been wrong. They closed at eight o'clock on the dot; the end of visiting time. Gazing towards the front entrance, the promise of fresh air lulled me outside. I made my way out of the black sliding doors hoping to see evidence of shops straight away. Almost immediately a cloud of sweet-smelling nicotine engulfed me. Even though I'd quit smoking years ago, sometimes a sheath of fresh cigarette smoke hurtled me back to those youthful days drinking and smoking freely in pubs. To my right, a heavily made-up couple huddled together next to an A-board in the ambulance drop off area. It was advertising a Lilliputian sized image of a frothing Flat White. The colourful tagline 'A taste worth waiting for' stood out on the cup. One of the girls had slightly puppyish shoulder length hair, wavy with a centre parting. She wore a tight white top with the words, 'Juicy Couture' printed sparkly gold, executed in a bold Old English typeface. The other tied her long dark hair back in a bun. She was dressed in denim shorts and a blue t-shirt decorated with 'Wish You Were Here' in yellow looping letters. They both smoked furiously. No-one was else around, and I tried making eye contact without success. Slightly embarrassed, I sought solace in my shoelaces for a moment. When I looked up, a magnificent peachy coloured sunset had ignited the sky. By contrast, a constant flow of traffic formed a lingering blur only a few yards away. I stood on tiptoe trying to see any shops but couldn't locate anything past the pedestrian crossing on the left or the set of lights to the right. About to head back inside, one of the girls glanced over in my direction whilst stubbing out her cigarette. I took a deep breath and tried my luck.

"Sorry to bother you ladies, but do you know if there are any shops open nearby?"

Juicy Couture nodded, "Kemp Town."

"Kemp Town…is that far?" I asked.

She was buried in her phone, scratching at the screen,

"Head over the main road down there and on to Paston Place. It'll only take a couple of minutes. Look out for the trumpet."

They looked at each other and giggled. Then a phone rang.

I took the crossing and found the road they mentioned. Looking back, it was almost directly opposite where I'd spoken to them. About halfway down, I started to hear a loud murmuring occasionally pierced by the odd shriek of high-pitched laughter. Getting closer to the noise, a curious shaped dome loomed into view. At first I thought it was a mosque. Then spying a throb of around 20-30 people gathered outside, I understood the trumpet reference. From a distance the building looked like a mini Royal Pavilion, with lotus-leaf ramparts strung along the parapet. It was certainly a unique thing to find hidden away along a backstreet, just one block from the seafront. Outside a youthful, scantily clad clientele fooled around in revealing negligees and Burlesque outfits. I couldn't decide which sight was more strange, the building or them.

Some hugged clutching bottles and tall glasses. A few even chased each other along the pavements surrounding what turned out to be the queue for a local cabaret. I edged round the main gathering to the corner of St. George's Road and headed towards a parade of shops about 100 yards further down. Inside St. George's News a group of teenage girls surrounded a Turkish looking man behind the counter. He was dressed all in black with tanned skin, almond-shaped eyes, and light brown hair. They were inspecting the e-cigarettes.

"C'mon, you must know how they work?"

I snuck carefully past and moved toward a couple of aisles that faced each other. Both lay behind a set of empty newspaper shelves. One was fully stacked with booze, the other had a limited selection of bland, expensive biscuits and brightly coloured plastic stationery. I grabbed two large bottles of Evian from the fridge and a smaller lemon flavoured Volvic. As I turned, a grubby guy with a toothless mouth came out of nowhere. He wore a long shabby check shirt and baggy combats. Catching me completely unawares he bumped right into my left shoulder. I stepped back narrowly avoiding the fridge. He made a low growling noise and I could tell by his grimace that he was trying to psyche me out. Regaining my composure, I decided against confronting such a hostile intrusion. I'd vaguely remembered seeing him with two other guys hanging around outside the entrance on my way in. Foolishly I'd presumed they were part of the group with the girls. Then when I thought about it for a second, I realised they hadn't said a word or acknowledged each other the whole time I'd been in the shop. I noticed how the combats guy made the Turkish man fidget uncomfortably on his stool. I took the longer way round the back of the aisles, allowing a couple of the girls to move ahead of me at the counter. They started pointing at the e-cigarettes again, twizzling the contents of the display case so that it reminded me of a rat scampering in a cage.

"I'm not buying one if no-one knows how to use it?"

As they renewed their discussion, I realised the girls were very young, sixteen at a push. Even so, the Turkish man looked through them, watching out in case the guy in combats blew his top at anyone. One of the girls, wearing a short black party dress and with a white and puffy face turned round sharply and pointed at the counter.

"You ever used one of these?"

I shook my head firmly, "Sorry, don't smoke."

Suddenly, a litre bottle of Smirnoff dive bombed in over our heads. Banged down with a loud thud, the sound of it reminded me of the Barista's milk jug at the service station.

"And a packet of skins!" a low voice snarled from behind us heading back to the drinks aisle. The Turkish man's eyes grew like saucers, moving in all directions trying to follow the other's movements. By now I'd had quite enough of the whole charade. I slapped a fiver down on the counter and shouted "keep the change," hurrying on my way out.

SLEEPING ELEPHANTS

I don't remember too much of what happened after I got back to the ward. We gathered round the bed again as time emptied itself out. Although the groans had receded, the breathing patterns had become much more erratic. Patting his left hand mother kept repeating…

"He's a fighter isn't he?"

After another long pause, I have to admit, I just wanted it all to be over. It was as if everyone had become hypnotized. Memories weighed more than stone in our long wait for the sun to descend. With the breathing gone cold, a final leg spasm left only the resounding silence of days vanished. Colourless as clouds before a storm, my sister trembled before she started to sob loudly. With that the nurses came.

I drove mother back to her house and she made coffee which we sipped quietly at the kitchen table. It was a difficult night's sleep. I kept replaying the final images at the bedside over and over. Desperately trying to replace it with something else, only the intricate pattern of the cabaret ramparts came to mind. In the end, I must have slept a little, because I woke up with the sun pouring in through the blinds. Turning over, I felt another painful twinge in my lower back. After lying still for a while, I decided to try getting up. Immediately a sharp, stabbing pain across the top of my head forced me back underneath the duvet. Eventually, I took a shower and made a mug of milky coffee with some buttered toast and felt a whole lot better. It was a bright, clear morning and mother announced she was taking the dog out. The time had come. With the prospect of cabin fever beginning to kick in, I decided to head out on my own.

On a steep bank leading to a bridle gate, a keen easterly almost cut me in half. It didn't stop me stumbling blindly up onto Telscombe Tye. A vast area of grassy down land, due to a common law right the Tye was often swarming with sheep and lambs from the nearby Stud and Kirby farms. This was much to the constant consternation of my folks and countless other dog walkers. I decided to head away from the coast in the direction of the Dew ponds, a familiar spot where I often lent on the surrounding wooden posts to watch dragonflies dance a shimmering iridescent ballet. Evenings usually brought rippling waves of swallows swooping and sewing their shadows together. After a gentle climb toward St. Michael's, an isolated farm keeping a silent watch over the open downs and heathlands, I paused to take in a view that glistened under my eyelids like a sigh. Fragments of sunlight skipped across the smooth rolling hills, resplendent with humplike shapes and soft velvety textures, reminding me of the Howgills that envelope Sedbergh. Exposed and scourged by the wind, I let a series of frantic gusts blow right through me just as the potent symbolism of Hemingway's 'white elephants' invaded my thoughts. The air grew thick as it moved across the fields under the shadow of a cloud. Engulfed in shade I tried to remember who had coined the term, 'sleeping elephants' instead. Overhead, a low pitched rasping sound filled the sky. I looked up and caught sight of an old biplane weaving a circuitous route out towards the sea. Its mazy patterns mesmerised for a while before another sound captivated me. It was the beautiful harmony of birdsong, rising as if in reply. A dash of skylarks hung in the air, while their relentless liquid warbles followed my every step. Slowly, I began to make my way down the other side of the ponds, following a sloping path in the direction of the seafront. The only other person in view was a woman dressed in a bright yellow mac with violet hair. As she approached, I smiled 'hello' at her, but she kept her gaze downwards. Still, I couldn't help but notice how the striking colours of her coat and curls contrasted with the whiteness of her face. Further on notices for lambing season had been nailed onto crooked wooden crosses, yet there was no sign of any sheep. I did though have to negotiate a mosaic of leftover dip strewn across the grassy meadows. Nearing the sea brought a familiar salty tinge to the air while the path was infused with chalk and the crunch of snail shells. Occasionally I almost surprised a handful of rabbits pushing their luck out on the open grass. I wondered whether a few nibbles were really worth the risk. I remembered how my father used to enjoy watching countless dogs poke their noses into the myriad of scattered burrows, often getting them stuck halfway inside. Thankfully, on this occasion the rabbits' distinctive white tails beat a hasty retreat at the merest hint of footsteps.

At the end of the bridleway I crossed over the coast road and onto the undulating cliff top. Here the grass was tough and longer as it swayed back and forth producing a golden shimmer, as if set alight. Eventually I took the steps down at the White Cliff Café and headed along the Undercliff in the direction of the Marina. It was high tide, so I decided to walk as close to the edge of the concrete ramparts as possible. Sometimes the spray flew up high in the wind before falling onto the walkway. I passed several parents coaxing their young ones into the firing line. As I walked on, screams of joy and laughter could be heard for long stretches interspersed with the rhythmic rumble of the ocean.

LA SCHIAVONA

I decided to stay on at mother's so I could help with the funeral arrangements. Surprisingly, my manager had told me to take all the time off I needed. I missed the distraction of work and often thought about how nice it would've been to spend some time in the opulent silence at Easedale Tarn. One of the first things I had to do was to visit the hospital and collect the medical certificate. I'd offered to go, as I thought it would be too much for mother to deal with. I found the office on the sixth floor, but didn't realise what would be involved during the meeting with a bereavement officer. After a short wait, I was ushered into a small room full of pine furniture and chairs backed with green felt. A woman with an earth coloured dress, round face and heavy set form held out her hand. She reminded me of the portrait of an unknown woman *La Schiavona* by Titian in the National Gallery. She sat at ease, her body slightly turned as she looked directly at me. An electric fan moved metronomically from side to side wafting occasional traces of perfume in my direction. She crossed her legs before going through a checklist of who I needed to contact. As she spoke, she kept putting her hand on my arm and gazed directly into my eyes. I soon began to tire of the overlong silences inbetween questions. Before long the whole thing started to get on my nerves, and I got the distinct impression that she'd almost expected to see a few tears.

"Tell me about what happened again" she said pulling a tissue from a pocket on her dress. I glanced at it and noticed some faint traces of lipstick.

"I wasn't there the whole time."

"I know it can be hard to remember anything about those last few hours."

"I guess so"

Then she smiled. "So mother's bearing up ok then?"

"I guess so"

"Now I know this isn't an easy thing for you all to deal with."

Eventually, she handed me her contact card. The next step at the registry office was a doddle in comparison.

My brother dropped by mother's frequently so that we could go and get a few quotes. The woman we met in the first funeral parlour had white wavy hair, like an old professor's. She wore a baggy cream coloured blouse and shapeless skirt. After shaking our hands she sat down and spoke with a breathless drawl, nodding her head slowly and constantly raising her eyebrows. A vast collection of imitation flowers formed a formidable barricade around her desk. After a while she handed over a price list with a host of items neither of us had even remotely begun to think of. Her sales technique relied heavily on repeating the same phrases over.

"I'm so sorry for your loss. It must be very painful for you and for your mother."

Halfway through, I began to stare out of the window at the tide of cars passing by on the coast road. Thankfully my brother did most of the talking.

"We'd like a cremation. Mum also said that she wants a religious service."

Curiously I didn't notice the lady write anything down, except for a few seconds right at the very end when she hastily started scribbling in a small notebook. The quote she handed over brought me back to earth with a bump. I could tell by the vacant look on my brother's face that we both had absolutely no idea how expensive these things were.

A couple of days later I went on my own to a

place situated a few doors down from the imitation flower lady's joint. This one was bigger, lighter and even contained a small room on the left of the main floor space with a couple of desks and chairs. After entering I stood unnoticed in the doorway for a minute or two, until a couple of staff looked up from their computer screens. They ushered me into the side room. As we sat down they hardly bothered to raise their heads or look at me at all. I noticed they were both dressed in black jackets. One wore pin-striped trousers and the other a medium length skirt. We sat across each other perhaps six or seven feet away on a long rectangular desk. Whilst picking at a scratch on the corner of her laptop, the one wearing pin stripes asked,

"Do you want us to just give you an idea of the costs involved or do you need it all written down?"

"I'd prefer it all on paper I need to show it to my brother." I said.

One of them coughed an acknowledgement and went to go and fetch a couple of pens. The hypnotic tones of a beautiful choral work graced the office, lifting the gloom during the wait for paperwork.

Thankfully a visit to the Co-op funeral parlour situated inside a neighbouring shopping centre rescued things. This time my brother and I were met by a tall guy; thirtyish wearing a tight charcoal coloured suit about two sizes too small. He guided us into a plain, square shaped room with dark grey walls, almost the same colour as his constricting suit. Before we sat down at a wooden table he offered us a choice of drinks. I asked for a strong coffee with plenty of milk, whilst my brother declined to have anything. When the tall guy came back he sat directly underneath the overhead strip lighting. He began to sweat and I noticed a reddish glow was coming off his closely shaved head, which looked a bit sunburnt. It didn't seem to trouble him too much. The more he spoke about their plan, his refreshing, no-nonsense attitude proved to be exactly what we wanted. Running through an increasingly familiar set of formalities, he encouraged us to do away with the traditional pomp of black hearses or large wooden coffins.

"More and more people are going for those covered with things like poppies made out of willow or bamboo."

As he finished his spiel he stood up and wiped the top of his head with a tissue. When neither of us said anything, he asked if we'd like the use of their chapel of rest service. I glanced at my brother who shrugged and held his hands out.

"Yes, I think mother would like that," I replied after remembering her say how much she would like to spend one last moment with him.

The guy nodded and loosened his tie before advising us to find some nice clothes and any personal items that we could put in the box.

After another short pause, he looked up toward the ceiling for a moment.

"You know the weird thing is, I'd never even seen a dead body before starting this job. At first it was a bit scary. And of course it can still be really sad at times, but I always find it very fulfilling."

I repositioned myself on the chair and asked what his friends thought about him doing this job.

A few wrinkles appeared through his sunburn as he laughed.

"Yeah, it can be a real party pooper. Some people

just can't handle talking about death. And I daren't mention about the embalming that I do. Especially given that's what really bumps up our wages!"

We returned the following day and were met by another member of staff named Rachel. She was busy talking on the phone so we stood back from her desk and loitered by the door for a moment. She sat in a high-backed chair in a more generous fitting charcoal grey suit that billowed out like a hot air balloon. On occasion her round face was lit by a warm, bright smile. She had a booming deep voice which took us both by surprise as it seemed so completely at odds with her smart appearance. After hanging up the phone she took out our file and announced she was going to be our 'arranger.'

"Don't worry; you can leave it all to me. And I'll look after mother on the day too. You'll have nothing to worry about. Plus, I've got someone in mind for the service. He'll be perfect - as long as he's available!"

Soon after, we paid the deposit and shook hands. The next hurdle would be bringing mother to the chapel of rest.

THE INFINITE HAZE

The thought of taking mother to the Co-op made me feel quite nauseous. Somehow, I knew it was my fate to do this. My brother said he had too much work to catch up with and I'm not sure where my sister was. When the fateful morning arrived we both sat silently on the drive for a moment. Just before I turned the engine over, mother said eerily,

"He knows we're coming, so there's no need to

rush." I switched the radio on and wound down my window a little. By the time we'd moved on to the coast road the sun was high in the sky. An annoying fly flew in on my side before it started buzzing in the bottom corner of the windscreen. In the end, I grabbed a CD case to waft it back out into the air. Belatedly we tagged on to the residue of the morning school run after going through the set of lights at the Texaco garage. I let a string of SUVs out much to the annoyance of the traffic building up behind. In between creeping forward, I stole a few glances out towards the azure coloured expanse. Nothing but a couple of sailing boats separated the sea from the infinite haze of the horizon's vanishing point. Unusually, mother kept relatively quiet. As we neared the centre's car park I could feel the blood pumping in my temples.

Once again, a different person greeted us at the reception desk. She held her hands together sympathetically before instructing us that everything had been made ready.

"Are you both going inside?"

I hesitated behind mother because we hadn't really discussed it.

"Would you like me to go in with you?"

She replied straight away, "Yes, that would be good."

Then the woman behind the desk chipped in,

"Well, make sure you take your time and if you need anything just let me know, I'll be out here."

I looked at mother but she'd glazed over.

"Don't worry, it'll be fine."

She nodded and straightened her jacket, before we crept down the hallway together past the square shaped room until the black chapel door loomed large like a standing sentinel. After a short pause, mother turned the brass handle and shuffled inside. I padded behind her into a small bright room, decorated with white flowery wallpaper. The faint sound of music wafted in above our heads. I wasn't sure what it was, as I was concentrating hard on avoiding eye contact with the coffin. I took a few deep breaths and fixated on mother instead. But she went straight over to it and picked up a couple of blackened fingers.

"Ooh they're so cold" she said grasping the tips even tighter as if trying to warm them up. The pine coffin rested on a long flat table to the right of the door. The lid stood up beside the doorframe and a name was inscribed on a shiny silver plate. There was no furniture. I thought it a little strange that they hadn't at least put out a couple of chairs. After standing idly in the middle of the empty room I decided it was time to turn round and face the music. What I saw didn't look like him at all. I don't think anyone looks like themself once they've died. His facial muscles no longer shaped the face and there was an overriding waxy finish to his appearance. At least he hadn't fully 'gone off'.

Somehow I knew the rather puny image of skin and bones would remain etched on my mind for a long time. At least he looked smart in the clothes we'd chosen for him. I knew he'd have approved of starting the big sleep in his favourite check green suit and tie. The shiny pair of brogues looked way too big in comparison to the rest of the shrunken body though. One final glance revealed that they'd carefully fixed a small badge onto a lapel displaying his beloved football team's crest. As mother seemed to be holding up reasonably well, I said I'd leave her to it before heading out. I didn't look back.

I'm not sure if she put anything else inside the coffin. She never mentioned it afterwards.

LEAVE, HUH?

I offered to drive mother and my aunt to the crematorium up near the racecourse on the outskirts of Brighton. This meant a small detour towards a tranquil residential park off the main south coast road adjoining Newhaven. My aunt's health had rapidly deteriorated over recent months due to the venous ulcers spreading from her feet and toes to just above her ankles. Now the only people she saw were the nurses who dropped by to change dressings. She'd become a hostage in her own home, relying solely on a wheelchair to move about. Typically, the last time I'd seen her was at another funeral on a cold, grey January morning some six or seven years previously. As I looked out of mother's bedroom windows at the soft, pure air, the morning's final breath lingered on the dewy grass. The garden, already full of the local harmony of birdsong was perfumed by incredible flowery, spicy and chocolate shades. A rainbow of hyacinths and clusters of blue clematis were beginning to speed away after latching on to a new piece of trellis.

It was already boiling by the time we set off, not long afterwards I had to pull over into a garage forecourt to take off my jacket, laying it carefully on the back seat. As we approached the residential park, mother turned and said candidly,

"I hope she's remembered. We don't want to be late."

I took a left into what appeared to be a labyrinth

of identikit homes.

"Blimey! What a maze... they don't look like trailers in the usual sense, but even so."

"You'd be surprised. Inside some of them are pretty spacious...2-3 bedrooms, fitted washer, dryer, some even have two bathrooms and a breakfast bar in the kitchen!"

"Weren't they called rabbit hutches though, because they were so small and had no storage space?"

Thankfully, after skirting the perimeter for a few minutes mother pointed at a unit on the right.

"There it is. She's left the door open."

"That's a big blue BMW blocking the drive!"

The handsome, muscular beast made my poor old Golf seem dull and drab by comparison. After pulling up alongside, I tried to peek in but the blacked out windows issued a stern rebuke. As we mounted the steps leading into a bright kitchen a murmur of voices trailed off inside. Catching a fleeting glimpse of someone wheeling my aunt around the lounge, I poked my head through a beaded curtain and coughed at the same time. My cousin gave mother a hug and offered a sweaty handshake. He seemed taller than I remembered with a large, pale and puffy face. Sweat soaked through his shirt as he reached up and pulled a glass from the cupboard above the sink next to the door.

"Took me over three and a half hours to get here from Birmingham this morning," he said inbetween gulps of water.

"Nightmare! It's good to see you though, been a fair few years."

I handed him an order of service and patted him on the shoulder.

The road to the chapel passed over a section of the racecourse below the main grandstand where an 11% gradient marked the sharp descent into the city centre. I had to take care negotiating a steep ramp after nearly missing a left hander signposted to the Crematorium about half-way down. The track eventually opened out into a bowl shape at the bottom of a long, sloping driveway. We arrived first in the waiting area on the right hand side. Withdrawn from the outside world, a sleeping militia of mock Victorian street lamps surrounded us. The manicured grounds enclosed by rows of silver birch, pine and yew trees were littered with grave stones of various shapes and sizes. Landscaped with care, a scattered garden to find solace and reflect on named benches walled in by iron gates and water features. The u-shaped red and grey brick chapel had an oval window that looked like a large wagon wheel. It was situated directly above an elongated pair of dark wooden entrance doors. There was a sign on a silver barrier post with a decorative top, 'Not open on weekends due to vandalism.'

As I turned the car round to face the entrance my brother and his wife pulled up in a swanky and sophisticated estate, the same make as my cousin's shiny German mean machine. My sister followed soon afterwards. In another fifteen minutes the car park had nearly filled. It was now approaching midday and the sun beat down relentlessly.

I stood exposed on the tarmac holding my aunt's wheelchair, whilst mother mopped her brow with a tissue and offered reassurances. I found it hard to see past the bright glow reflecting off the row of bonnets so I went to go and take a look at the flowers in the Garden of Remembrance. They were laid out in a shaded area next to the heavy chapel doors. After padding over to a piece of shaded ground, I bumped into a cousin-in-law. He looked sharp in a pair of nicely cut trousers, a decent white shirt, and black polished Chelsea boots. Only a statement beard gave away his true status. His mind seemed more preoccupied with the forthcoming referendum.

"Have you decided yet?" he asked.

"You know the more I hear, the more I'm inclined to vote Leave."

"Leave, huh - you serious?" I replied.

He stood still for a moment, silent, reflective, and then he smiled.

"Guess so…You can't get away from it. It's on the TV and radio all the time. Besides, there's no debate about any of the *real* issues. All they ever seem to do is just slag each other off."

"That's politics for you, complete waste of time," I said.

"Be careful what you wish for though. Remember those lying bastards will say anything to get your vote."

My brother hurried by in a blur and threw his hands up. He was urging everyone to head toward the small waiting room just inside the main doors. As we made our way over, I noticed a crowd of around ten people obscuring the doorway. The Chaplain stood apart from them, a few yards to the right. He looked most excellent in a suit decorated with military medals on his lapel. He also wore a black coloured robe, like an academic. I wandered over to introduce myself and shook his hand firmly. We stood in silence on the steps for a moment. He kept looking at his watch and shaking his head.

"Ah, here come the pallbearers" he said.

When I looked up I couldn't see any sign of Rachel our arranger though. Instead, a young guy dressed in a three-piece suit, with striped trousers and an enormous top hat introduced himself as Nathan the Co-op's representative. My brother caught up with us, just as the Chaplain ran through the order of service one final time. He asked if we would like to assist the pallbearers carry the coffin into the chapel. I turned and looked at my brother who shrugged and said nothing.

"Of course, it would be much better if you could" the Chaplain added.

He nodded slowly and left us alone. The organ struck up and most people took the cue to go and take their seats in the chapel. Suddenly a hoarse, rough wail broken up with a sort of choke cut through the sombre chords. At roughly the same time, a nebulous canyon of clouds formed overhead dimming the light in the dark corners of the entrance steps. For a moment the baby's repetitive sobs echoed like the final hours at the hospital. Meanwhile, the Chaplain headed back in our direction.

"I'm sorry to have to press you both, but have you decided yet?" he gripped hold of my right arm as he spoke.

Desperately, I searched for a point of reference amongst all the white noise, eventually settling on the pallbearers who murmured obscene endearments to each other.

The time had come.

I looked at my brother deaf now to the distant

voices dropping down into dust.
"What's the matter?" he asked.

www.ingramcontent.com/pod-product-compliance
Lightning Source LLC
Chambersburg PA
CBHW011958090526
44590CB00023B/3772